GET THE
RIGHT
JOB!

GET THE
RIGHT
JOB!

From Writing an Effective Résumé
to Negotiating a Fair Salary,
a Practical Guide for Confidently
Navigating Today's Job Market

JEFF MAGNUSON

© Jeff Magnuson, 2019
Edited by Jordan Eagles
Cover art and design by Kostis Pavlou

ISBN 978-0-9990982-9-5

To all the current and future job seekers

GET THE
RIGHT
JOB!

Contents

1

Why This Book Is Necessary and What It Will Do for You

Searching for a new job, whether you need one or want one, can be stressful and difficult. I want to help you. This book is meant to guide you through the uncertain, oftentimes frustrating, process of looking for a new position.

Times Are Changing

The current professional landscape is not the same as it was in the 1980s, 90s, or even the early 2000s. Substantial shifts are happening within companies and the overall job market which continues to make job searching challenging.

Previously, people went out after college and looked for stable companies to work at for 30 to 40 years. Once they were "in the door," they would then climb the "corporate ladder," get pay raises, more responsibility, and then retire with additional steady income from their pensions.

Those days are long gone, except for a small group of people. For almost all of us, the corporate ladder is extinct and company (and employee) loyalty is not valued the way it used to be.

Of course, this does not apply to every single company out there, but it's rampant enough where you will very likely find yourself in the larger group, if you're not there already.

A second reason why job searching in today's world can be taxing is that there is no shortage of advice out there; either in books or articles, from friends, co-workers, parents, and other family members. Within that advice is a lot of conflicting information as well as lingering "old school" thoughts which are not only outdated, but potentially <u>detrimental</u> to you and your ability to job search effectively today and beyond.

Note: There is one exception to this that we'll cover in Chapter 6.

It was after hearing much of this advice over the last few years, while also witnessing the further shift in the job search culture and studying more about it, that I developed my own point of view that best captures how job seekers (You) can effectively use your limited time to set yourself up for the best chance of finding the right position.

Yes, the *right* position. You deserve a job that fulfills you, gives you opportunities to grow, and pays you a fair salary.

It's Time to Think Differently

As a career consultant, my number one request from job seekers is how can they <u>stand out</u> from other candidates when applying for jobs. It's a great question and is also the premise of this entire book.

If you want to stand out, **you must think and act differently** from the majority of other job seekers out there. And, as you will soon see as you go through this book, I am not talking about monumental changes, but rather small, subtle shifts that mostly have to do with your own mindset. There are other changes that are more visible but these adjustments are neither dramatic nor frightening, yet will yield significant results for you.

Who This Book Is For

Generally speaking, this book is for anyone who wants a fresh perspective on the whole job search process with strategies and tactics that work. More specifically, it's for students looking for summer internships, students getting ready to graduate, recent graduates, professionals thinking about making a job change either now or in the future, and professionals currently out of work.

Through a combination of direct advice and intriguing stories[1], the information contained in these pages is meant to *empower* you by giving you a wider understanding of how a lot of the job search scenarios work. This, in turn, will help prevent you from getting hung up on any one sticking point and allow you to stay focused and positive until you find your next opportunity.

Note: Some chapters will include popular questions I receive when I advise people. I have put these questions in bold and italics.

---

[1] The personal details and scenarios have all been adjusted for anonymity. You can rest assured, however, that all of the stories in this book are true. In fact, I'm sure you have your own stories that would fit into some of these scenarios. My hope is that you take comfort in knowing that it's not just you who sometimes has to deal with "funny," head-scratching moments when job searching.

Like this?

Yep, just like that.

Additionally, I wanted this book to be only as long as necessary. I know how time-consuming job searching is, especially when you're working full-time and/or have other responsibilities. Everything contained in these pages is important. I've cut the content down to the bare essentials so you can spend more of your time job searching effectively with the information contained within.

Goals

My goals with this book are to:

1. Help you grow and develop your confidence.

2. Help you understand many different facets of the job search dynamic from multiple perspectives.

3. Tell everything to you straight.

4. Help you watch out for the pitfalls along the way (because there are plenty).

5. Provide you with a blueprint of how to manage your time to find the right job for you.

6. Provide you with all the steps that will be needed leading up to you signing your offer letter.

Topics

Specifically, we'll cover the following topics in this book:

1. How the job market has changed and why that matters to you now and in the future.

2. How to write an effective résumé and cover letter.

3. How to optimize your LinkedIn profile and use it to your advantage.

4. How to proactively apply for positions and get noticed by the right people.

5. How to handle third-party recruiters ("headhunters") and what to look out for.

6. How to prepare for phone, online, and in-person interviews.

7. How to negotiate an appropriate and fair salary, and much more.

So far in my career, I have been an employee, a hiring manager, a job seeker, an MBA graduate, a career switcher, and a career coach. Career coaching is a passion of mine and there is nothing more satisfying than getting feedback from a client about how these steps gave them the confidence to not only seek, but land the job they really wanted.

I want the same results for you.

I have experienced a lot so far in my career and I stand behind everything I'm about to share with you in these pages.

Writing this book was a joy and I hope you find the same value that others have found by both changing your mindset and following these easy steps.

Let's get started.

2

You Are in Control

Aside from the general changes to the employment landscape over the last 20 or so years, it's important to understand right away that the job search process is largely inefficient and incredibly annoying. If you've recently job searched for any length of time, you know what I'm talking about.

This annoyance creates a larger issue because it gives current and future job seekers hesitation about venturing into this mission, even if it ultimately means improving their professional lives.

If more companies were attentive, they would realize they are doing *themselves* a disservice by making the hiring process much more cumbersome than it needs to be. However, this book is not for them, it's for you. Changing processes across thousands of companies is not going to happen that quickly, so we need to work with what we have and what we know.

Besides, complaining about how broken the system is will not help any of us achieve our goals; however, acknowledging this up front is necessary as many job seekers put a lot of pressure on themselves at various stages in their search when a lot of the causes of their frustrations are completely out of their control.

Why We Dislike Looking for New Jobs

Many people dread the thought of having to look for a new job for a number of reasons. While many of these reasons have merit, the negative mindset that results from these reasons is what really makes the whole job search process seem daunting.

Here are four reasons why people dislike looking for a new job, whether they are forced to or not:

1. Uncertainty. Many companies, and sometimes third-party recruiters, do not provide enough transparency during the process; leaving candidates wondering if and when they are going to hear back on their interview, offer, or candidacy status.

2. Unhelpful, weak advice. Advice along the lines of "work isn't supposed to be fun, that's why it's called work" and "companies are in control, that's just how it is" exacerbates the negativity.

3. Low confidence. Much of this stems from job seekers not understanding their true value and instead relying on other's opinions of them, even potential employers who do not know them well, if at all.

4. Complacency. It's understandable for employees to be content in their current roles and not want to change, yet...

Complacency Can be a Killer

One reason is because many employees still believe their companies will take care of them indefinitely as long as they do a good job (old school thinking). Unfortunately, this is a dangerous assumption to make. I'm not suggesting that a company is intentionally trying to harm employees in any way, but what I *am* saying is that when companies need to make tough decisions (usually financially driven), it's not uncommon for even solid employees to be laid off.

Additionally, it's comfortable to be comfortable. I get it. I don't know about you, but I've made a lot of great friends over the years with people I first met at work. While that is a wonderful thing, you cannot let your office friendships get in the way of your professional career. If you're really friends with your co-workers and consider them a part of your extended family, then that will not change. You will still socialize with them outside of work.

Don't forget that companies are not taking your comradery, however meaningful, into consideration when they need to make difficult decisions. When it comes to your livelihood and working at a deserving company that pays you fairly and treats you well, you need to take any emotional attachment to your current job out of the equation.

Story: There was a 2018 article about a U.S. food manufacturer that laid off hundreds of employees as a cost-cutting measure. The company's sales were steady but, by eliminating those employee salaries and benefits (expenses), the company could maintain a stable profit margin.

Was this a personal attack on those employees? Of course not. It's a business, and if companies can look at it that way and let employees go with little remorse, then you can (and should) do the same thing when it comes time to improving your personal and professional situation.

Remember, your relationship with your company is a **business relationship**—a professional connection where each party has a personal interest to either protect or advance, sometimes accompanied by a formal agreement—treat it as such.

You are the *only* person who can effectively manage your professional life. You must take active ownership over all aspects of your career, whether you are currently employed or not, as you are the only one who ultimately has your best interests at heart.

The Job Seeker/Company Dynamic

For too long, job seekers have been seen as inferior to companies that are looking to hire. This can be either directly, based on how job seekers are treated, or indirectly, by this unspoken "understanding" that a company has all the power and, therefore, job seekers are to do as they say.

More specifically, I see four main reasons why many job seekers have this *perception* of companies having the upper hand:

1. Companies get large amounts of résumés for whatever positions they post. As we will discuss in Chapter 6, this is meaningless as many, if not most, of those résumés are often not a good fit for the open positions. Additionally, many of the submitted résumés are never even viewed by someone at the company.

2. External recruiters. "Headhunters" have been a part of the job search dynamic for years. I have devoted Chapter 7 to these folks as it's important to understand how to effectively work with them.

What I will mention now, as it's critical to know, is these recruiters are paid by the *companies*, not you. Therefore, in order for these recruiters to keep their clients (the companies), they often need to accept whatever the company is demanding of them, regardless of the confusion or inefficiencies it may create for you and/or the job search process.

3. Employees used to stay with companies for decades. As previously mentioned, one company used to be a big deal to an employee and his or her long-term goals.

4. Companies have the money that you need. Your bills and other expenses don't stop just because you're out of work or unhappy in your current role.

Job Seekers and Companies Are Equals

Let me now breakdown why companies that are looking to hire professionals and professionals who are looking for new positions are equals.

The technical answer is that the résumé submission → job interview → signed offer process is a **business transaction**. In order for a transaction to work, *both sides* must agree, otherwise nothing will happen; the company will not get its new employee, and the job seeker will not get a new position.

The better answer lies in how we look at the job seeker/company dynamic. Job seekers tend to solely focus on the hiring process from *their own* perspective and all the stress and uncertainty that comes along with it. However, as I just mentioned, there are two sides at play here.

Let's look at the hiring process, generally speaking, from a *company's* perspective.

Companies hire based on their **needs**, not their wants. Every legitimate job opening must be discussed and approved beforehand as new hires are a significant expense for a company. Once a position is approved, the company then has the time-consuming task of finding the right candidate.

Finding new employees is often stressful for companies, especially the hiring managers, particularly if they are desperate for help.

For example, if a hiring manager's team is already stretched thin, then a larger attrition risk on his team could be a possibility if the personnel openings are not addressed promptly. If that should happen, then there is another risk of that allotted headcount being withdrawn because of a temporarily frozen or permanently cut budget. If that should happen, and more employees leave, then the department could be at risk as very few managers will want to have to rebuild and retrain a brand-new team while also trying to move their business forward.

Therefore, if you approach your job search with the insight that a company does not hold all of the cards in this dynamic, because of its own needs and potential risks, then you can understand that both sides have a lot to gain from each other.

This is the first of many small mindset shifts I mentioned in the opening chapter. It's simple and effective. *Good* hiring managers are not mythical creatures dangling an open position to whomever they deem worthy. No, they are stressed out professionals who *really* need to find the right person to make their team whole again or perhaps start up a brand-new team with bright and capable professionals.

The Best Time to Start Is Right Now

Note: This section assumes you are currently working. If you are not currently working, fear not, as the content here will still be beneficial to you.

Working a tough day and job searching at night is not an ideal situation by any stretch. However, many professionals make the mistake of waiting to begin their search when their current job starts to negatively impact their daily lives, while others don't start until they find themselves without a job. Neither of those scenarios benefit you because instead of being in full control, you are now working against time to find something else while the bills keep coming in and your stress level rises.

The best approach for everyone is to start looking when one or more of the following scenarios occur:

1. You find yourself wondering if there is anything better out there.

2. You realize your job is not as fulfilling as it used to be (or as you thought it would be).

3. You don't see any advancement in the near future.

4. You sense a change, or tough times, ahead for the company which could directly impact you.

5. You are stressed out and often dread the thought of going to work.

Let's dissect these.

#1 - #3. If you've been in a role for a reasonable length of time and you're bored, first speak with your manager to see how you can expand your responsibilities and/or try something new. If you're doing a good job at work, you deserve the opportunity to grow. But you have to take the initiative. Do not assume that your manager will automatically do this. Your manager is busy with many things as well as focused on her own career and may not realize your situation and how you feel until you bring it up. It's your career. Speak up!

If you get the sense your manager is either unwilling to help or doesn't see much advancement or change for you, politely thank her and then continue doing your job like you were before. Then, at night or on the weekends, update your résumé and LinkedIn profile and start searching around online for other opportunities that may interest you.

The Signs Are Everywhere

#4. Whether you work in an office, on a factory floor, or somewhere else, every location has a structure and a routine that develops over time. Colleagues have their schedules and tend to come in around the same time every day, eat lunch with the same people, and typically leave around the same time. Interactions and banter among co-workers become fairly common. There is an energy that becomes consistent in the workplace, a flow.

Pay attention to when that energy starts to change. For example, when a new manager is brought in, the group dynamics can shift and relationships can change. But what about when the company starts to have mediocre or negative financial results? In rough times, you've seen friends and colleagues suddenly laid off while others seem to "retire" out of the blue.

Story: Several years ago, a company that people really enjoyed working at changed dramatically. Led by upper management decisions, many employees noticed several small changes that snowballed into a major office culture change. In one example, goals at the end of the year, which bonuses were tied to, were set impossibly far out of reach. Matching retirement contributions were now being paid in July of the following year. This meant if you were not employed prior to this payment date, then you would not have your company's matching contribution, despite working the previous full year. Routine personal time to pick up children or visit the dentist were now being tracked as vacation time. This all culminated one winter during a dangerous snow storm. Employees were warned that they would not be paid for the day if they left early to avoid the traffic. Aside from being plain cruel and unprofessional, especially since employees could easily work from home, this edict posed a safety issue as several employees had difficulty getting home when they left at the end of the day because of the hazardous road conditions.

This is what I'm talking about when I say negative changes. All of the above happened at one company over a period of a year. Things were not always like I just described, but they *became* this way because of deliberate choices by senior leadership. Many employees quit and moved on to better and healthier organizations.

If you sense a negative change in the environment and you and your co-workers are not as happy as you once were, or you notice that management is having a lot of meetings that you're no longer invited to, or your annual review was blatantly inaccurate or unfair, don't ignore those signs. Pay attention and get your résumé and LinkedIn profile fully updated and be prepared to start looking for a new position somewhere else. If things improve for you at work (new title, responsibility, general environment, etc.) then you can always put your job search on hold for a while.

#5. Your professional situation and its effect on you is as important as your physical health. Think about it. When you're really sick for more than a few days, what do you do? You listen to your body and go to the doctor.

If you're in a toxic environment where your confidence is slowly being eroded and you're experiencing symptoms such as loss of appetite, grinding your teeth, constant headaches, bad moods, and/or anxiety, then it's time to assess your current situation and, most likely, make a change. Again, this change could be at your current company or, if they are not willing or able to help you, at a new company. Don't assume things will get better in your current role or that you need to grin and bear it. Your mental health and your professional career are incredibly important and need to be given the same care and attention as your physical health.

Finding Your Next Opportunity Starts with You

Once you decide you're ready to move on to a new position, whether you're currently working or not, there are specific steps you need to take in order to use your limited time effectively and not get overwhelmed and/or discouraged by the whole job search process.

When times are tough, looking for a new job with a positive attitude and a truck load of confidence can seem almost impossible.

It's not impossible.

If you switch your focus and place the extra energy that you're spending on stressing out about your current company into finding a better solution, then at least you will be taking steps to make the change you need. The key is to take it slow, one step at a time. Keep the road ahead manageable by doing a little extra work each week to set yourself up for a positive change.

Start with 20 minutes a day for three days a week; either before work or at night. That's one hour of progress toward improving your professional life. In that amount of time, your résumé and LinkedIn profile can be substantially improved, if not fully updated; an enormous first step.

If your current job has become disappointing, use it for what it has been reduced to—an income source—while you use your free time to learn about other options and begin taking steps to see what else may interest you.

Four Questions

Every six months, take a few minutes and ask yourself the following four questions:

1. Where am I in my professional life?

2. How do I feel about my situation?

3. Where do I want to go next?

4. How do I go about achieving this next step?

The answers to these questions are specific to **you**. You don't have to share them with anyone. It's your life and your career and you get to decide how you feel about your present situation without any outside opinions.

Something as simple as taking stock of where you are and how you feel at any moment is incredibly powerful. I recommend doing this at home, on the weekend, when you're relaxed and not distracted.

Regardless of whether you've received positive or negative feedback at work, you are still entitled to make a determination about your current employment state by taking everything into account including your:

1. Work

2. Manager

3. Salary

4. Benefits

5. Commute

6. Co-workers

7. Happiness

8. Future

You have to understand where you are and where you want to go *before* putting a plan in place to get there.

Tip: If you are unsure about what you want to do next, use job search websites and start reading as many job descriptions as you can. Type in some search terms (i.e. marketing, retail, accounts payable, communications, etc.) and see what populates. Read the descriptions and if you see something interesting within in the postings, then enter *that* new word or phrase into the search field and see what new jobs populate.

Keep in mind that no one will know you're searching; nor should they. Don't mention your job search to anyone unless you trust them completely. The last thing you want is for the wrong person or people to find out, possibly putting your current employment at risk.

Confidence

Before we wrap up this chapter, there is one topic I need to touch on more closely; confidence. Confidence is the secret sauce to this entire process. Confidence is a tricky thing because it's dynamic and falls on a long spectrum between having a mountain of conviction at one end to feeling completely useless at the other end. Confidence also triggers emotions in us that directly impact our daily lives.

Many job seekers, especially those who are unemployed, can quickly find themselves in a low confidence state of mind. It's important to understand that job searching takes time as companies often move very slowly which is, of course, out of your control. Furthermore, your skills and self-worth are not diminished during the period in between jobs, even though it may feel like it at times.

You have an enormous amount to offer a company whether you've been searching for a day, a month, a year, or more. Stick with me here and realize that these insights and recommendations were written based on my discussions with hundreds of job seekers. You are not alone in how you feel.

Confidence is power and when you approach job searching from a place of power, your mood will improve, your attitude will improve, and the positive energy you bring to interviews will shine through.

You need to take control of your career starting *right now* and that includes taking stock of your professional life while you are still employed, even if things are going well. Taking control, and then realizing you're in control, will keep your confidence strong.

In the next chapter, we will start to get into the nuts and bolts of this book, beginning with the cornerstone of the entire job search process, your résumé.

3

How to Write an Effective Résumé

Your entire job search begins with your résumé. It's the foundation of how you present yourself to human resource (HR) professionals, hiring managers, third-party recruiters, and the general public (via LinkedIn). Your résumé serves **one primary function**: to get you an interview.

Your LinkedIn profile and cover letters will be based off of your résumé, as they will all need to fit together and be consistent based on what you want to pursue. We'll cover those topics separately in the following two chapters.

Until you no longer need it, your résumé is a *working document*, meaning it's never actually finished. Whatever your latest version looks like right now, is how it looks right now. Your résumé should be revisited at a minimum of every six months for updates and/or refinements. This does not take a lot of time but is an important exercise as it benefits you in the following three ways:

1. If you are unable to add a new bullet point from your current job, then you need to speak with your manager and figure out a way to do something new at work. Showing progress is key on your résumé and in your professional life.

2. It's easy to forget some of your achievements at work with many other distractions occupying your time and thoughts. By putting in the effort two or three times a year to update your résumé, you will ensure it's the best version it can be. This is critical because your résumé, when written properly, will be branded for the next step in your career. Your career history will be written to lean in the direction you want to go; allowing your résumé to clearly demonstrate why you are a good candidate to interview for a particular role.

3. Having an up-to-date résumé ready to send to someone on short notice is good practice as you never know when opportunities could present themselves. Sometimes companies need or want to move quickly in order to fill positions. If you have a résumé that you can turn around to someone in a day or so, you will make a great first impression.

Take the Time

You never want to rush through writing your résumé. Any mistake on a résumé, however small, is a potential red flag to an employer. These documents must be 100% polished and error free. If you scramble to throw one together at the last minute, you open the door to having a mistake and/or a weak version.

I've written countless résumés and well-written ones take time; as in several hours. Think ahead and take the time to thoughtfully write your résumé so it is up to date and ready to go, while also being disciplined enough to revisit it every six months to ensure the document is in top shape.

The Keys to a Good Résumé

We were all told at some point in our lives how to write a résumé, as if there is only one acceptable way to write these documents. There isn't only one way, despite what some people may tell you. In fact, there are <u>no rules</u> when it comes to résumés which, while I personally think is a great thing, can confuse and overwhelm a lot of job seekers.

The reality is that there are only opinions and preferences when it comes to writing résumés. What I will demonstrate in this chapter is what I believe to be an effective use of the page or two dedicated to letting other professionals know about you.

Note: In general, be very skeptical about any advice that comes with absolute terms (i.e. "This is how *all* résumés *must* be written."). There is no one correct way to approach many of the topics in this book.

Before we dive into the details of writing an impactful résumé, let's first examine the document from a higher level, like we did with the job search process in the last chapter.

Once again, many job seekers only think about their résumé from their own perspective. The better way to think about these documents is from the point of view of the person you are trying to reach; the **hiring manager**.

You need to make it crystal clear (painfully obvious) to the hiring manager why she needs to consider you. You do not want to rely on her to try and piece your work history together to decide if you're a good candidate for interviews. Do the leg work and *show* the hiring manager why you should be interviewed at the company.

This approach is important because hiring managers are busy people and they, based on many articles written on the topic as well as conversations I've had with dozens of professionals, do not spend a lot of time, sometimes only *seconds*, reading résumés. Of course, this does not apply to every hiring manager and HR professional out there but it's common enough that we can assume your résumé will not be viewed for very long.

I know that's disheartening to hear, but it's also helpful to know. And while we're not going to convince everyone to spend more time reading résumés, what we *can* take away from this is to implement an approach that takes this valuable information into consideration.

Let's now go step-by-step through the entire résumé and talk about what you need to include, what to omit, and how to format it to make the biggest impact to your audience.

Overall Layout

From a layout perspective, keep it simple and straightforward. Some modern résumé templates make the document look like a confusing puzzle. You want your résumé written in such a way that it's easy for someone to either skim quickly or read more carefully.

Also, stick with serif fonts, such as Times New Roman and Cambria, as they are professional looking fonts; perfect for résumés.

Name and Contact Information

First and foremost, your name is the largest font on the résumé and goes in the top center of the page. Right underneath that, in a standard font size that matches the rest of your résumé, goes your home city/town, state, phone number, email address, and LinkedIn URL.

For example:

Jane Example
Park Ridge, NJ · 999.999.9999 · jane@example.com · www.linkedin.com/in/jane-example

Note: For this book, those fonts are smaller in order to fit properly on one line. On your résumé, the font size for your information will match the rest of the document.

Notice how your full home address along with the words "phone" and "email" are omitted? It's not necessary to include that detail. Specifically, for your home address, there are too many ways for people to search and make judgments about where you live if they know your address. Keep your résumé simple and leave off that detail. You will provide your address and other relevant information to HR when the time is appropriate.

Note: For your email and LinkedIn URL, use hyperlinks so anyone can easily click on them to either email you or check out your LinkedIn profile.

Summary

Next is the Summary. This is vital to your résumé, yet many professionals do not have one. Please note that this is *not* an Objective Statement, like you may have seen in the past. The Summary goes deeper than a simple one sentence objective.

The Summary is similar to an Executive Summary at the beginning of many company presentations, only here we're going to provide the reader with a high-level overview that illustrates who you are, what you enjoy and/or excel at (possibly including a recent accomplishment), and what you want to do next. That way, if one were to read nothing else except for your Summary, they would still have a snapshot of you in just a few sentences.

Here are two examples:

Project Management Office leader with 10 years of client-focused experience in the IT Industry. I have a diverse portfolio of successfully completed complex projects with a specialization in the development and continual improvement of technology project management processes and strategic alignment to larger organizational goals. I thrive in environments where I can effectively communicate with clients and partners to streamline and execute organizational changes.

I am currently seeking a Project Management opportunity where I can leverage my background and skills to lead large-scale iniatives and deliver results on time and on budget to meet a company's critical business needs.

I am a marketing professional with over 10 years of experience planning and executing various marketing and communication strategies to build awareness and generate sales. I have routinely collaborated with dozens of cross-functional partners to develop, execute, and analyze impactful campaigns that have supported dozens of dairy products across multiple categories.

I am currently seeking a Senior Brand Manager position where I can leverage my experience, skills, and passion for driving brand visibility to lead a team to develop and implement meaningful programs that propel consumer demand.

Experience

Next comes your experience in reverse chronological order. This approach is not something new or innovative but it makes the most sense and is what résumé readers are accustomed to seeing. Your latest positions are, arguably, your most relevant to what you are looking to do next, therefore, that information belongs at the top.

The company is in bold font and your job title is in both bold and italics. Before going right to the bullet points, add a brief sentence or two about the company and your general role there. This is especially important if you work at a small or regional company. Again, make it easy for your reader and tell them about the company. Don't assume they are going to research companies they have not heard of before.

Here are two examples:

HIJ Company, Los Angeles, CA | Jun 2017 – Present
Senior Consultant. A Toronto-based, start-up, fashion eCommerce company, I was hired to help set up its operations in Los Angeles, including partnering with shipping vendors, to build critical business development.

TUV Corporation, Jacksonville, FL | Nov 2016 – Feb 2018
Territory Sales Manager. Brought in to this frozen food manufacturer to manage all of the distribution, including the third-party brokers, in a 6-state, Southeast region.

Bullet Points

This is where your <u>achievements</u> and <u>accomplishments</u> go. The tendency for professionals is to list their main day-to-day tasks and responsibilities instead of their highlights. Day-to-day tasks do not tell hiring managers *why* they should hire you. When too many job seekers simply list their tasks, then every candidate starts to sound the same, and no one stands out. This, in turn, becomes a massive headache for hiring managers.

Companies do not have the time to interview everyone and have to be selective when determining who to bring in for interviews. Differentiate your résumé by adding your own achievements that are <u>unique to you</u>, and you will elevate your chances of being called for an interview.

Note: These do not need to be massive accomplishments. If you made your team, your manager, or the company better in some way, mention it proudly!

Note 2: Make these *measurable* by showing data, if possible. Not every role lends itself to achievements that can be shown numerically (and that's totally fine), but try to illustrate your results as best you can.

Avoid Short Sentence Fragments and Add Pronouns and Articles

The other point of differentiation is so simple, yet few job seekers do it. This approach is to write your résumé using full sentences (or expanded sentence fragments) and not short sentence fragments that only start with a verb, like we were originally taught.

Résumés written with short fragments are difficult to read and usually do not flow from one bullet to the next. Reading résumés written in this way is exhausting because nowhere else in the English language do we speak, read, or write in constant sentence fragments. Therefore, we shouldn't be writing our most important professional document this way either. Don't be shy about adding pronouns and articles such as "I," "we," "the," and others.

I thought we should never use "I" or other pronouns on our résumé?

This goes back to what I mentioned earlier about there being no rules. In the past, the general advice was no pronouns and only short sentence fragments. Times have changed. Make you résumé more readable by using pronouns and explaining why your achievements were/are so important.

Please realize that you will not be making your résumé too wordy by doing this. Listing only day-to-day tasks is what makes a résumé run too long. This expanded approach makes it more *readable*.

By using full sentences, or expanded sentence fragments, your résumé will be easier on the reader and will increase the likelihood that he or she will *want* to read more of your résumé to learn more about you and your work history. Make it interesting.

Bullet Point Comparison

Let me illustrate this point with examples. First, here are a few bullet points written in those short sentence fragments:

- Creating and monitoring content calendar.

- Provide strategic leadership by suggesting improvements, alternatives, and upgrades.

- Identify prospective leads and share with the sales team for the follow-up.

- Managed business operations from manufacturing to distribution.

- Develop content that produces calls-to-action to our website.

- Processed and fulfilled wholesale and direct-to-consumer orders.

- Planned and handled logistics for trade shows and consumer events.

- Monitored and resolved all customer issues.

Imagine you're a hiring manager and you receive a résumé that contains bullet points like the above. Those bullets do not tell you nearly enough about a candidate to help you decide if he or she should be brought in for an interview over someone else.

As a candidate, you must work to ensure that the time a hiring manager spends looking at your résumé is meaningful and gives him a sense of who you are (and why you're great) so he decides to pick up the phone to learn more about you.

Next are a few examples of bullet points stretched out to include more substance:

- Led the effort to transition to a new fulfillment vendor; significantly improving our operational efficiencies and the customer experience while reducing our costs by 25%.

- Saved the company over $2MM in 2018 by negotiating cost reductions with the local union in several service areas of our hotel properties.

- Crafted and designed strategic fundraising emails and campaigns, including our end-of-year giving, reaching over 40K constituents and increasing our total fundraising by 45% over the prior year.

- Exceeded my annual quota by an average of 125% by meeting with 3-5 clients per day and educating them on how our company's service offerings will greatly benefit their organizations in both the short and long term.

- Reduced our costs by 50% in 2016 (as part of a 2-year long project) by sourcing new suppliers, renegotiating contracts, and optimizing current costs with our 200+ contractors.

See the difference? Yes, the bullets are longer than the original list but they are so much more helpful to the reader. Showing your achievements and accomplishments will make the hiring manager's job much easier which, in turn, will increase your chances of getting the interview.

Note: Use actual numbers in your résumé (i.e. "3," not "three") as people's eyes are drawn to numbers more quickly.

No Generic Terms

Avoid using those hollow phrases that seem to show up all the time in various places. Phrases like "results driven," "solutions oriented," "hard working," among others are meaningless. Those phrases can literally apply to any job function in any industry. Instead, talk about your accomplishments and **be specific**. What solutions did you come up with? What were the results of the big project you led? How did you go above and beyond to help the company? Paint a picture for the reader by telling short anecdotes.

When you combine interesting sentences with relevant and meaningful information about you, your résumé will stand out.

Education, Skills, and Interests

Next comes your education, skills, and interests. The *one* caveat here concerns those who are either current students or recent graduates of either undergraduate or graduate school. If that's the case, then your education will go at the top of your résumé, above your current or most recent employer.

Note: For those of you out of school for at least ten years, remove the graduation dates from both your résumé and your LinkedIn profile. The dates are no longer necessary.

Note 2: For recent undergraduates, go ahead and list either your overall or major GPA if it's above 3.5, as well as any honors (i.e. Dean's List). If not, just leave them off. After 3-5 years of work experience, you can remove your GPA and any other college activities you participated in. None of this extra information will "harm" your résumé, your professional experience will simply weigh more heavily for future roles.

I really don't want to mention my personal interests.

I understand and I'm not suggesting you share anything that gives you even a little hesitation. I'm only speaking about fun interests you wouldn't mind sharing.

The purpose of including some interests is two-fold:

1. Your personal interests will give your new résumé even more personality and will let a hiring manager or HR professional know a little more about you before you even speak to her.

2. The interests provide talking points for a potential conversation that have nothing to do with your previous employment history or the company you're interviewing with. This is important because if you are speaking with your potential manager, and he values the *person* he will be working with, then these interests can be used to trigger some friendly dialogue.

There is a big difference in the tone of a conversation when you're answering formal questions versus when you're answering questions about the best book you've ever read. Good managers want to hire people who they will enjoy working with, so put a few fun things that you like to do at the bottom of your résumé as it can only benefit you and possibly be the difference between you getting the interview or even an offer.

Note: Keep it light. Things like cooking or baking new recipes, exercising, reading mystery novels, and playing softball are harmless, but interesting activities. If you like to hunt or gamble or are into other polarizing hobbies, keep them to yourself. Don't list personal interests that some people may not be comfortable with.

Story: A client of mine only had a few things she felt she could include; one of which was hiking with her dog. I told her that was totally fine and added it to her résumé. Guess what happened? She and her future manager spent five minutes talking about dogs during her interview. Now, I obviously can't say for sure if that was the reason she got the job, but what I can say is that it helped her in a positive way because they were able to quickly form a personal connection during her interview.

Here is an example of the bottom section of your résumé:

Education | Skills | Interests

Rutgers University, New Brunswick, NJ
Bachelor of Arts; Economics

Proficient in Microsoft Office Suite, Photoshop, InDesign, WordPress, MailChimp, and Google AdWords.

I enjoy playing soccer and skiing, attending live music events, reading biographies, and cooking Italian dishes.

Putting It All Together

Here is a condensed version (only two companies listed) of a full résumé. You can find additional samples on my website (www.jeffmagnusonconsulting.com/sample-résumés).

Roger Example

Boise, ID · 999.999.9999 · roger@example.com · www.linkedin.com/in/roger-example

I am a Human Resources professional with 15+ years of experience in the manufacturing industry. I specialize in change management, company branding projects, cost containment, and talent selection. I am a demonstrated leader with proven success in developing effective teams, facilitating training programs, and creating strategic recruitment plans.

I am currently seeking a senior HR position to utilize my leadership and experience to build and strengthen a company's employee processes, training programs, and overall efficiencies.

JKL Company, Seattle, WA | Dec 2016 – Present
Director of Human Resources. Recruited to guide JKL's management of their HR operations, systems, and programs. Partnered with senior management to create new policies and procedures.
- Successfully opened our Seattle office; recruiting employees, creating group benefits, and developing robust training programs.
- Saved JKL over $2.5MM in 2017 by negotiating favorable contracts with health providers.
- Established an on-boarding program for all new HR employees joining the organization; a first of its kind for JKL.

PQR Corporation, Portland, OR | Dec 2014 – Nov 2016
Human Resources Manager. Based on my success at my previous
position, I was promoted to manage a wide range of HR efforts
including recruiting and training employees, administering
benefits, and overseeing all HR records.

- Saved the company $35K in 2 years by implementing an
  internal employee review system; reducing our dependence
  on an outsourced contract.
- Collaborated with recruiting teams to create initiatives to
  drive the flow of diverse candidates into the Operations
  division. Our efforts resulted in a 25% increase in diversity.

Education | Skills | Interests

Rice University, Houston, TX
Bachelor of Science; Communications

Proficient in Microsoft Office Suite, PeopleSoft, Cornerstone, Taleo,
PeopleClick, Bartech, and LinkedIn Recruiter.

I enjoy volunteering, tutoring ESL, practicing yoga, reading horror
fiction, and painting.

Look

Every single person, when they open a book, magazine, menu, etc.,
makes a split-second judgment of how something looks. Same with
your résumé. If the page is filled with copy and very little white
space and looks like it's going to be a slog to get through, you're
immediately at a disadvantage. On the flip side, if the margins are
really wide and there is too much white space, your résumé could
come off as light or weak, visually speaking. The key is to find the
balance, so a reader wants to read it and can then do so easily;

whether they are skimming the document quickly or reading it more closely.

Length

Should all résumés only be one page?

As a general rule, keep your résumé one page or less if you've been working for ten years or less. If you cannot get your information comfortably onto one page (possibly because you've had several positions), that's okay. Let the résumé spill onto a second page. Most printers print double-sided, so your information will not be lost if someone prints your résumé out. Plus, you'd rather your résumé be evenly spaced on one and a quarter pages than crammed onto one page.

Almost no one's résumé needs to be more than two full pages long. There are exceptions for certain academic résumés (CVs) or senior executives, but generally speaking, keep yours brief. Don't forget that you'll be able to share additional stories during your interviews, so not everything needs to be on paper. Let the résumé be your highlight reel.

Old Positions

Your résumé is your marketing document, not a legal document. Don't be afraid to leave old positions off of your résumé. The part-time job you had in your teens and twenties can disappear once you add a couple of newer positions on your résumé. Additionally, if you've been working for a while, those first few jobs you had 25 years ago are likely no longer relevant. Take them off.

You are not obligated to list every job you've ever had, despite possibly receiving that advice in the past. If anyone demands to see all of your work history, explain that you are happy to share your relevant experience. If they persist, find another company to apply to or another recruiter to work with. Neither of those parties are worth your time.

Note: This is especially important for job seekers who are concerned about age discrimination which, unfortunately, is a real thing in today's world. Two easy work-arounds are:

1. Leaving the dates off of your education

2. Not listing every position you've ever held

Neither of those pieces of information are required, so keep them private.

Proofread

Make sure your résumé is mistake free! Read it over slowly and carefully. Print it out and read it out loud. Read it backward (i.e. the last sentence first, the second-to-last sentence second, and so on...). Make sure the bullets are vertically in line and your margins are evenly spaced. Double check that your contact information is correct and that your email and LinkedIn hyperlinks work properly.

Finally, always send your résumé (and your cover letter) as a PDF, not a Word document or some other document that can be manipulated or edited (unless you are asked for a specific format). PDF documents look more professional. When including a cover letter, keep the PDF as one document, so the cover letter is the first page and your résumé is the second and, if needed, third page. When applicable, make the recipient's job easier by having them only open one attachment and not two.

Multiple Versions

Very often, clients of mine have interests beyond their current career path. This is great! You should push and stretch yourself professionally, however, don't assume you can use the same résumé for every job type. If you are interested in different types of positions, then you need to have multiple versions of your résumé. These versions do not need to be completely different, but each one must show you in the best light for the position you are applying for.

For example, if you are interested in moving from a traditional external sales role into an internal customer service type role, there are many crossover skills that will work to your benefit. The idea is to highlight more of those and less of the unique sales skills for this desired customer service position.

At a minimum, your Summary will need to be updated to reflect what you are looking to do next, so your résumé doesn't say Sales Professional when you're applying for a Customer Service role. Also, make sure the sentence or two about what you're good at or enjoy doing fits with the new role. Finally, don't be afraid to swap out (or add) some bullets to your résumé that align with what the new job is looking for.

For example, if the new job is looking for someone who can multi-task and you have an accomplishment that highlights that trait, then be sure to add it to your résumé. At the same time, if there are bullets that make your résumé confusing for this new position, simply remove them. This résumé would then be your "customer service" résumé.

No one will know you have multiple versions of your résumé except for you. Label them accordingly and keep track of the version you send to each company. It's not a lot of extra work, but it's important that you show a company you are 100% interested in them (and their specific role) and then back it up with a solid résumé and cover letter that demonstrates your interest.

Sound good?

We've covered a lot of information in this section. Consider re-reading this chapter when putting your résumé together to ensure you have all of the sections completed properly. I have also included a checklist in the Appendix of this book for you to use when writing your résumé.

Let's now move onto another critical component of your career search, your LinkedIn profile.

4

Why LinkedIn Is Important (and Easy to Set up and Use)

If you are not on LinkedIn yet, the time has come to set up an account. If you are on LinkedIn and use it regularly, the following information will sound familiar, however, there may be something here that's new or helpful to you as well.

For those of you not on this platform or if you have an account but do not use it regularly, hear me out. Your reasons for either not wanting to have an account or use the site often are valid, but let me explain why staying fairly active on this site, especially when job searching, is in your best interest and can increase your chances of finding your next position.

LinkedIn, as of December 6, 2018, has 590 million users![2] Generally speaking, this site is unlike many other social media outlets. The content skews almost entirely toward the professional landscape,

---

[2] https://www.omnicoreagency.com/linkedin-statistics/

across multiple industries. You can choose to follow or connect with whomever you want including friends, colleagues, companies, brands, public figures, and general topics that interest you. You can browse quietly or more publicly, add your voice to conversations, and even write your own articles. You have complete control of your profile on the site and how people see you on it.

You can learn about companies and get inspired by the amazing amount of success stories and thoughtful posts that are uploaded daily. You can do much of your job search right on the website, via the "Jobs" tab, or on their mobile app; discovering roles you may not have thought of when you first started your job search. Thousands of companies list their open jobs on LinkedIn and you can easily find hiring managers and/or third-party recruiters and, just as importantly, they can find you.

Note: LinkedIn does not replace networking and meeting people in person to develop meaningful connections, but can certainly help you establish those first connections, which are most helpful when searching for a new job. In fact, if there is a position you are interested in, absolutely reach out to someone "cold" to see if they would be willing to speak with you informally about the company. They may even offer to pass your résumé on, but don't go in with that expectation. Just use this platform to try and learn what you can so you can then decide if you would still like to apply.

The most important thing to do first is either create a new, or update an existing, profile. The website does have a tutorial that walks you through where and what to add to your profile, but let's quickly cover all of the elements in more detail here.

Your Profile

Setting up a profile does not take a long time, but it's in your best interest to have it fully updated before you start reaching out to people in or out of your network. You want to come across as polished and professional and this does not take much effort on your part. You want the public's first impression of you to be a positive one and all you need to do is follow these simple steps to have a professional looking, updated LinkedIn account. Feel free to also use mine as a rough guide (www.linkedin.com/in/jmagnuson).

1. Headshot – Absolutely post a clear, smiling, up-to-date photo of yourself. This photo should be from your shoulders, up. Anything more than that and your face will be too small in the space provided. Your LinkedIn profile and your photo are how you will be seen by many for the first time. People are attracted to smiling, positive faces, so make it a great first impression!

Having a photo also shows that you take your profile seriously. Other people want to know, and are generally more comfortable knowing who they are talking to and/or who is leaving comments. A headshot gives them a better idea of who you are.

Note: You do not need to spend money on professional headshots. Take a crisp selfie in good, natural lighting. The picture will be cropped close anyway.

1a. Background or banner photo – Not as significant as your headshot, but it rounds out your profile nicely and anything is better than the default banner image on LinkedIn. Get creative and give your page a little personality (while keeping it professional) with a unique banner photo.

1b. Contact information – Not everyone is able to contact you directly through LinkedIn, however, if you list an external email, and make it public, then you will give people who are not directly connected to you, but who do have a LinkedIn account (such as recruiters) the ability to reach you without having to first make contact on the site.

2. Headline – Very important, especially if you are out of work and actively job searching. A clear headline tells anyone who comes across your profile (whether directly on your personal page or in a search result) *exactly* who you are.

You may hear people talk about keywords and why they are important. Keywords are important here because anyone, including hiring managers, can do searches on LinkedIn. You are limited to 120 characters, so your headline needs to be very brief and to the point.

If you are openly job searching, then you should use phrases like "in search of," "seeking new," and "open to new opportunities" among others in your headlines. For example:

- *Operations Director Currently Seeking New Opportunities*
- *Project Manager in Search of Marketing Manager Opportunities*
- *Sales Representative Open to New Opportunities*

Recruiters and hiring managers know to search for these words and phrases, so use them to give yourself a better chance of being spotted in a search. Also, as you noticed in the second example, use the headline to branch out. This is why I included the more specific *in Search of Marketing Manager Opportunities*. It's your career. You get to decide what to pursue next. And, once you do decide, plainly spell it out so others know as well.

If you are currently working, put what your current position is and leave out the part about searching for new opportunities. This is especially important as, chances are, you do not want anyone where you currently work to know you are actively looking for a new position. The headline will be a giveaway so be very careful about what you do or say because most of it will be visible to the public.

Note: You can make all of your LinkedIn settings private but if you're searching for a new position, I do not recommend doing this. You want people to be able to see you and reach out with potential opportunities.

One word about what not to put in your headline. Some professionals choose to put either nothing or irrelevant words and/or phrases in their headlines, such as:

- *Experienced Strategic Leader*

- *Business Professional*

- *Living the Dream*

- *Marketing/PR/Sales*

- *Ivy-League-Educated*

Don't waste your valuable headline space with meaningless or generic words. And don't leave it blank! You need to stand out immediately. Phrases like the above will not pique someone's interest. Those people will likely just move on to a more clearly labeled profile. Use your headline to your advantage and let other professionals know exactly who you are.

3. About/Summary – Here you have more room to expand upon whatever you would like to focus on. If you are openly job searching, then you can reiterate that you are open to new opportunities as well as provide the reader with a lengthier write up of who you are, what you enjoy/are good at, and what you are looking to do next. This will be very similar to the Summary at the top of your résumé except here you can magnify certain areas and go into more detail about a big project or your current situation, if it's relevant.

Note: In "Your Dashboard," you have the ability to select "On" in the "Let recruiters know you're open" line under the "Career Interests" section. This is mandatory if you are currently out of work and actively seeking a new position. If you are currently working, you can certainly switch this to "On" as well, just be mindful that there is no absolute guarantee that your current employer will not see this, so proceed with caution. Adding the relevant keywords and information to your Headline and About sections will already increase the chances others see your profile.

4. Experience – Many companies have their own LinkedIn pages so when you start filling out your work history, the company will most likely populate. If the company is not on LinkedIn, that's okay, you still can, and should, list the name of the company. The only items that will be missing are the company's logo and information, but that's not a big deal.

Your LinkedIn profile is a subset of your résumé. For each position, write a few sentences about the role and what you accomplished there or list two to three bullet points. Do not copy and paste your entire résumé into the field. Keep it short and sweet and let people then reach out to you to learn more.

The positions on your LinkedIn profile should match your résumé. Therefore, as discussed in the last chapter, if you decided to leave certain old jobs off your résumé, leave them off your LinkedIn profile as well.

Also, I do not recommend posting your full résumé document on LinkedIn. Your résumé is a very personal document and you want to be able to control who has it. It's not a good idea for it to be forwarded around without your knowledge. If someone is interested in you after seeing your profile, he or she will be able to contact you either through LinkedIn or via your public email address.

5. Education – This section is pretty self-explanatory, but let me mention a few points. First, as mentioned in the last chapter, do not include your graduation dates on your profile once it's been ten years since you've graduated, or if you are older and just recently graduated (as a general guide). Your age is no one's business and your degree is just as valid if you earned it yesterday or twenty-five years ago. Keep the dates off.

Extra-curricular activities that you did while in school, once you've been out for five or more years, are not really relevant anymore. They won't hurt your profile but it's just something to keep in mind.

6. Skills & Endorsements – I personally do not know many people who pay too much attention to this section but if you're on a connection's profile, you can certainly endorse him or her for whatever skills you'd like. It's a nice gesture that may even get reciprocated.

7. Recommendations – These are important. We no longer put "References furnished upon request" at the bottom of our résumés and I don't imagine too many people have updated letters of recommendation on file. What we *do* have are LinkedIn recommendations. If you have three or four people who you are comfortable asking for a recommendation, please consider doing this sooner rather than later. Recommendations give your profile a tremendous lift and no one can post a recommendation without your consent, so you can review their words (and suggest changes, if necessary) before posting their recommendation to your profile.

Note: If you're currently working and you ask a colleague, vendor, or customer for a recommendation, please make sure you trust they will treat your request as confidential. Be aware that making such a request is sometimes seen as a giveaway that you're starting to look around for a different job.

8. Be active to increase visibility – The more you "Like" and/or comment on posts, articles, and news stories, the more your name will be seen on your network's feed. For example, if you like a particular blog post, what will likely happen on several of your connections' pages is they will see "Jane Doe liked this" above the article that is now appearing in their personal news feeds. I can't say how the LinkedIn algorithms work, but suffice it to say, the more you do this, the more visibility you will have.

Note: Increasing your visibility increases the chance of someone reaching out to you but keep in mind there is also such a thing as too much exposure and people can turn off notifications from you. Therefore, use your discretion when liking and commenting.

Finally, any comments you make will be public so be very mindful about what you say, especially about sensitive topics, as you never know who may read them.

9. Be aware about who you connect with – As with any social media channel, be careful with whom you interact. If someone starts behaving in a way that bothers you, you can easily block that person and they will no longer be able to access your page. Also, be aware of anyone asking for personal information. If you feel a ping in your gut that suggests a person may not be trustworthy, ask questions or get them on the phone. Any person who really wants to help or work with you will make the time. Otherwise, ignore them.

LinkedIn cannot police all the bad players. You must be vigilant when using the site.

Finally, be cautious when connecting with people with whom you currently work. Many professionals are not comfortable connecting with people they work with as they want to keep their LinkedIn activity separate from their work life and colleagues. That's understandable. The last thing you want is to be actively job searching (even quietly) and have a colleague notice and then start telling other people. Keeping your profile private will certainly help with this effort, however, it also makes it impossible for others to see you, like recruiters and hiring managers.

Note: This is a good time for me to quickly mention your other social media accounts, if you have them. There is a chance hiring managers or others will view any public pages you have. Therefore, if you have unflattering pictures or ones that could give someone pause, consider deleting them or, at least, untagging your name from them. Additionally, you can always make your other social media accounts private, so they're only visible to whom you designate. The last thing you want is to give someone a reason not to consider you for a current or future position.

Regardless of how you choose to use LinkedIn, please recognize how powerful the site is and how it can positively help you and your career. Use it cautiously, like you would anything else, and start building and/or expanding your network while learning about and pursuing new opportunities.

Let's now move on to another document that will help you get a hiring manager's attention, the cover letter.

5

A Cover Letter Matters

A properly written cover letter can serve as a great opportunity to stand out from other applicants.

Before we dive in, let me first acknowledge a few reasons why many job seekers do not like writing cover letters:

1. They don't like talking about themselves

2. Cover letters take time to write

3. Writing them seems like a waste since many companies never seem to respond

I understand all of those reasons and more. In this chapter, I want to help you craft a concise and effective cover letter. Then, in the next chapter, we're going to talk about how to get your cover letter and résumé in front of the right person, so the time you put into each document does not go to waste.

The fact that many job seekers really dislike writing cover letters means that many applicants either skip writing them entirely, use a generic one, or write one where they only talk about themselves. All three of these approaches are ill-advised.

Writing an Effective Cover Letter

Keep it simple; two-thirds to three-quarters of a page **max**. Whoever gets your cover letter will not want to read a long letter but will more than likely read a relevant, concise, and compelling one.

The first item on the page is the date. Place it in either the upper right-hand or left-hand corner. Follow this with a space and then the hiring manager's name and job title followed by the company's address; just like with any formal business letter. Examples can be found later in this chapter.

Note. Normally, you would put your home address at the top of a business letter but, just like with your résumé, you are not going to include that detail here.

Note 2: In the next chapter, I will show you where to find the hiring manager's information.

The first paragraph states who you are and why you are writing to the company. This can be in response to a specific job posted or because you have an interest in the company even if there is no job posted. Yes, you can (and should) do that if you're really interested in a particular company. More on this at the end of the chapter.

The next paragraph, which is separated by a space, contains a line **about the company** and any recent news you have uncovered in your research. For example, a mention about their new product line you've seen in your local store or maybe a recent acquisition you read about. This is immediately followed by what you think the issues are for the hiring manager. They all have them, especially when they are looking to fill roles. Get out in front of it and make a guess either based on the job description or the recent news you mentioned.

This approach shows initiative on your part. You are taking the time to not only research the company but to also think about what must be going on in the department that they need *your* help.

Here are two examples:

Given the recent acquisition of XYZ Inc. and its vast assortment of products, I have to imagine there is a need to not only integrate the products into your company's larger portfolio, but to also develop and execute a cohesive marketing strategy to build recognition for this new-look product line.

ABC's remarkable annual results in the fintech space, along with your anticipated growth outlook, will require professionals who are not only technically proficient but also team players so on-going improvements throughout your clients' organizations can continue to be anticipated and implemented.

In the next paragraph, you should illustrate a personal business achievement of yours that has some parallels to the issue(s) you mentioned in the previous paragraph.

When I say illustrate, I mean tell a very brief, *specific* story of how you achieved or accomplished something that made your current or previous role better in some way. It is so much more interesting for the reader and also allows you to infuse a little personality into these typically dry letters. As mentioned in the résumé chapter, this does not need to be some monumental project that was talked about in a press release. If you worked on something that made your company better in any way, talk about it.

Here are two examples:

During my time at XYZ, I continuously worked to raise sales velocities and overall brand awareness using various social marketing strategies, especially ads on Instagram. Through sharp photos, fun videos, and likeable dialogue, we cultivated meaningful engagement which brought a younger consumer base to the brand.

In the summer of 2015, I was at *The Summer Program for Kids* where I worked with children with emotional disorders and taught them about medication management as well as social and emotional coping skills. My efforts there allowed me to partner with the director at Florida State University the following summer to successfully develop and execute a summer program for their *Social Skills Program*.

This is powerful because you're now making it clear to whomever is reading your letter what you can do for them if brought on board. And you're doing this by showing them what you have already accomplished.

Finally, express your interest in wanting to learn more about the role and the company.

End it.

That's it. Interesting and to the point. You are putting a portion of the focus on the company and the hiring manager to create an engaging letter.

Here's a hypothetical cover letter that brings this all together:

February 17, 2019

Ms. Sandra Smith
Senior Director, Planning
Widgets, Inc.
625 First Street
Austin, TX 12345

Dear Ms. Smith,

My name is Betty McNamara and I am writing in response to the **Senior Manager** position that I saw posted on LinkedIn earlier this week.

I have to imagine with the company's growing range of luxury goods, there must be a need for someone with the experience of not only working with complex supply chain systems, but who also has the ability to communicate and train best practices to colleagues.

My experience in retail management, along with my accounting degree, aligns with your need for the right candidate to continuously improve the ordering and inventory monitoring processes at Widgets, Inc.

Last year, my two direct reports and I identified and removed over $250K in excess inventory while seamlessly managing 125 existing SKUs and several new items.

I am currently looking for an opportunity where I can leverage my experience to continue to grow my career and I welcome the opportunity to learn more about your company.

My contact information can be found on my résumé on the next page.

Thank you for your time.

Sincerely,
Betty McNamara

Short, simple, and right to the point. No fluff. No generic nonsense.

Most job seekers do just the opposite; they talk about themselves and their skill sets, sometimes for multiple pages.

Do not do that. A hiring manager is unlikely to take the time to read a very long letter that just talks about you.

Do the extra research and *show* hiring managers why you are worth speaking to about their specific needs.

Okay, I got all that, but these still take time and I'm busy. Why can't I just use a generic cover letter instead?

HR professionals and hiring managers can sniff out generic cover letters in two seconds. If you've ever had to read cover letters, chances are you can spot them pretty easily, too. It's a wasted opportunity and, more importantly, can actually make your first impression a negative one.

Take the time to do a little research about a company to show your interest. This approach will help you stand out from dozens (if not hundreds) of other applicants.

Applying to Companies with No Positions Posted

There is no reason why you cannot send in your résumé to express your interest in a company. When I said in Chapter 2 that you must take control of your career, this is another example of what that looks like in practice. There are no rules here. If there is a company you're really interested in and you don't have a contact who already works there, then you can still send in your résumé. Worst case? They read and discard it.

You never know where a company might be in their hiring process. Maybe they are getting ready to make a hire and post the position. Maybe they have the money to immediately hire a consultant. Also, a good hiring manager knows how time consuming and difficult it can be to find really good people and perhaps he or she will want to have coffee or a brief informational interview with you. After that, you can very likely find yourself top of mind should something open up. You will also have a new connection for your professional network which will only benefit you.

Here is an example of what a cover letter might look like for a company that does not have a current open position listed:

January 25, 2019

Ms. Charlotte Davis
Vice President of Marketing

Corporation of America
57 Main Street
Warwick, NY 12345

Dear Ms. Davis,

My name is Fred Armstrong and I am a big fan of your products. In fact, I was thrilled to read about your new blueberry-infused olive oil taking first place at the annual culinary awards last month.

I have to imagine with the tremendous competition in your categories, along with shoppers tending to spend less time in the center store, there must be challenges with continuing to grow your consumer base. Introducing new products is certainly one way to face those challenges head on.

During my time at ABC Corporation I helped develop and launch over 15 new products. Additionally, I continuously worked to raise sales velocities and overall brand awareness using a wide range of digital and traditional marketing strategies while staying within our budget. Many of the initiatives we implemented over the years helped drive double digit growth across multiple categories. The brand's success helped fuel the substantial growth in the category.

I would welcome the opportunity to speak with you further about Corporation of America and your products as I am open to new director-level marketing positions at this point in my career.

My contact information is on my résumé on the next page.

Thank you for your time.

Sincerely,
Fred Armstrong

Cover letters are even more important if you are trying to move into a different area from your current role. In this case, use the cover letter to show why your past experience makes you a great candidate for the new role. Most professionals have skills and expertise far beyond what their current job title and job description suggests. I'm willing to bet that you have a story or two of an achievement that has many parallels with your desired position. Once again, make it easy for the hiring manager to make the connection by spelling it out for him or her.

I'm always a little discouraged when I take the time to write and submit a good cover letter with my résumé only to never hear a thing. It would be nice if there was a better way to apply.

Wouldn't it? The next step is an essential part to the whole job search process and is all about getting your new résumé and your relevant, thoughtful cover letter in front of the right person.

Let's move on.

6

How to Apply to Positions Going Forward

Have you noticed that despite all of the new technology and websites that make it easier than ever to apply for jobs, you still rarely know if anyone even saw your résumé and cover letter?

While the online portals do make it easy for job seekers, they also make it difficult for companies as they can get inundated with sometimes hundreds of résumés for a single position. Since it's so easy to apply, many job seekers, even those who are not a fit for the position, think "Why not?" and submit their résumés online. This now leaves HR folks with the impossible task of sifting through piles of résumés which can, understandably, lead them to either quickly scan them, or worse, not read them at all. This puts you at a disadvantage because your résumé is not standing out among the numerous mediocre ones.

Networking

If you know someone at a company, and are comfortable doing so, absolutely reach out. The reason why so many professionals get new jobs by having a contact at a company is because it saves the company a lot of time and also removes some of the uncertainty about how a candidate will likely perform. After all, from a company's perspective, when they hire someone, there is always that unknown factor of whether the new hire will work out in the long run, even if he or she interviewed well. Networking and then subsequently getting referred by an insider helps eliminate a lot of the unknowns for a company and a hiring manager.

If you don't know someone at a company that interests you, that's okay! We're now going to go through all of the steps to give you the best chance of first getting the interview and then landing that offer letter for the job that interests you.

Sending Your Résumé and Cover Letter *Solely* Through Any Online Channel Is Not Good Enough

Don't be fooled into thinking you're applying to numerous positions if you're just applying online. When you only apply online, your name either sits in a queue with dozens of other names, where it has a small likelihood of being read or even seen, or is sent through a company's Applicant Tracking System (ATS)—computer software that scans your résumé to decide if you're eligible to move onto whatever their next step is, based on pre-programmed keywords.

Perhaps unsurprisingly, the automation of reviewing résumés is upon us. It's not a perfect system and, thankfully, you don't have to be at its mercy. Nevertheless, there are many job seekers out there who immediately want to try and beat the system with proper keywords and phrases for the ATS software. As a consultant, I get this request a lot.

Let's first understand that no one, other than the employees at a company who have access to the software, knows what exact keywords or phrases a company is looking for. Therefore, there is no sense in trying to guess and then overloading your résumé with many keywords. Additionally, with so many job seekers *already* taking this exact approach, many résumés are continuing to sound exactly the same. This leaves companies in the same place they've already been, which is why writing your résumé in a way that highlights *you* is so important.

You have to move away from the online-only approach as it's not designed to work in your favor.

Improve Your Odds

What I am trying to help you do is take methodical steps to increase the *likelihood* that your résumé will be seen by the right <u>person</u> and then get called in for an interview.

You need to use an approach that some of us used to have to do years ago, which is to use the United States Postal Service to deliver hard copies of your cover letters and résumés right to a hiring manager's desk.

That's right, folks. It's time to party like it's 1992 and break out the large envelopes and stamps. I'm talking 9-inch x 12-inch large, white envelopes.

Your cover letter is one piece of paper and your résumé is a second piece of paper (print on both sides if your résumé content is over one page). Staple them together, sign your cover letter, neatly hand-address the envelope, use two stamps ($1.10 total as of this writing), and mail it off. If you have more than two pieces of paper or if you are mailing outside of the United States, then the postage will be over two stamps.

This. Approach. Works.

Why?

Because professionals get very little regular mail at work anymore; and when they do, it's mostly catalogs or junk mail.

How?

By finding the hiring manager's name and the company's address and then sending your résumé and cover letter directly to that person.

Easy Steps

Whether you are interested in a position that is formally posted or you want to apply to a company that interests you, you are going to use LinkedIn to find out who the hiring manager (your next manager) will likely be, and then send your documents directly to him or her.

Follow these steps to locate the probable hiring manager for the positions you are interested in:

1. Go to the company's page on LinkedIn.

2. Click on the link that brings up the list of all employees at the company.

3. Click on "All Filters" and scroll down to add the "Title" of the next level up from where your title would be. In other words, your future manager's title. For example, if you are a looking for a Manager level position, search for Directors. Directors search for Vice-Presidents (or vice-verse, depending on the industry), etc. If you cannot find anyone one level up in the department you are interested in, then go two levels up.

Eventually you will find a name that makes sense for you to send your résumé and cover letter to. If you send it to the wrong person, there is still a good chance your information will find its way to the correct person at the company.

Note: LinkedIn will sometimes show the hiring manager for certain posted jobs. This isn't always the case but be aware this step may already be done for you.

To find a company's mailing address, just go to the company's "About" section on their LinkedIn page or do a simple online search.

Shouldn't I just send my résumé and cover letter directly to HR?

No. You want to send it to the person who has the real need (unless you are interested in HR roles). HR may have a list of open positions but it's not realistic to assume they have a handle on every detail for every position. The hiring manager knows who she specifically needs better than anyone else. Find *that* person and let her take the steps to get the company to contact you.

Note: In some cases, finding the hiring manager will not be possible. This can be either for remote positions outside of an office or because the person is simply not on LinkedIn. In the event that you cannot find the hiring manager or an alternative, mail your information to HR so at least someone in the decision-making chain is reading your cover letter and résumé.

Keep Track of the Letters You Send Out

Now that you have all of the elements for your letters, be sure and keep track of where you are sending them along with the names of the hiring managers in a spreadsheet or notebook.

This is important because the idea is to start sending several of these letters out each week and it won't be long before you lose track of which companies you're applying to. Also, when someone from one (or more) of the companies contacts you, you can easily go back and reference what the position is (and what résumé version they received) before getting back in contact with them.

One of my biggest frustrations is never hearing back from companies after I apply. Will this approach change that?

It's important to note that there is a difference between companies that do not contact candidates who <u>apply</u> versus companies that do not contact candidates after they <u>interview</u>. For now, let's only talk about not hearing back after you apply.

As mentioned, companies get flooded with résumés and even though yours will show up as a hard copy, it's unrealistic to expect to hear back from every or any company if they are not interested.

What you can take comfort in is knowing there is a good chance that the <u>right person</u> actually saw your résumé and made some type of decision.

Most likely, the hiring manager:

1. Wasn't interested and threw it away. Great!

2. Was insulted because you skirted the system and contacted him or her directly. Great! You don't want to work for someone like that anyway.

3. Passed it onto HR for consideration. Great!

4. Passed it onto HR with instructions to contact you. Even better!

5. Contacts you directly. Ideal!

Hoping or expecting to hear back after you apply is another waste of your time and energy. While the professionally courteous thing for companies to do would be to let you know, the reality is that they are not going to necessarily take the time to do so. In either case, it's out of your control.

You will never know exactly what happens to your résumé once it goes out the door, and that's okay. You're going to handle this with the final step of this new approach, which is:

Move on to the next opportunity. *Do not wait* on any company or any person. Ever. Keep researching. Keep sending out résumés. Keep moving forward.

From now on, you need to treat job searching as a realistic numbers game, with significantly improved odds, and work to give yourself an advantage over other job seekers by taking a better approach. You have your tracker to keep yourself organized. Just keep searching for new, exciting opportunities and work to get your résumé and cover letter in front of the right person at all of the companies you're interested in.

This seems really time consuming.

Sending quality résumés and cover letters takes time. Don't overwhelm yourself. Set a realistic goal. If you are currently working, try starting with three cover letters and résumés a week and increase it if you can.

Break the whole process down into manageable chunks of time. For example, search for positions on Sunday, Monday, and Tuesday and mark the jobs you want to look into further. Then, either on those same nights or during the middle of the week, research more about the positions and the companies, including the mailing addresses and names of the hiring managers. The end of the week can then be reserved for writing out your cover letters. That way, when the weekend comes around again, all you need to do is give the letters one last proofread and off they go.

Keep in mind, the more cover letters you write, the easier this will become and the less time you will spend on each letter.

Finally, for those of you currently <u>not</u> working, try sending one or two letters out *a day* as you'll have more time to research different positions and companies.

Yeah, but I can apply to more companies if I just apply online.

Yes, you can, but, like I said, those are not quality applications. Those are lottery tickets with terrible odds. By taking the time to methodically contact companies you're interested in, you will increase your odds of landing an interview and ultimately finding the next great job in your career.

So, should I not apply online at all?

You should, but only after you have sent out your résumé and cover letter in the mail. Since you have already done the work, you might as well submit your information electronically as well. Take the extra few minutes and apply on whatever online portal they are using.

Note: If they have online applications, don't spend *any* time re-typing your résumé into those fields. Just make a note that your résumé is attached. If a lot of fields are required, then don't bother at all. If a company should contact you because they received your hard copy and they then ask you to fill out their online application because they're interested in you, go right ahead. You now have their attention which was the goal.

Job Descriptions

Before we move on to the next chapter, I want to address a real sticking point for many job seekers; company job descriptions.

If you've ever felt hesitation about applying because you couldn't do (or have never done) several of the tasks listed in a company's job description, then today is the last day you are going to worry about that. Most of the job descriptions we are used to seeing are unrealistic in their entirety. In other words, the candidate who matches everything a company desires (at the salary and experience level) often times, does not even exist.

Here are some of the reasons why we have to endure these job descriptions:

1. Too many people are involved in writing the job descriptions. Very often the hiring manager, or someone on his team, initiates the

process followed by HR and a higher-level manager; each adding their own bullets to the job description.

2. Companies use outdated descriptions instead of reviewing and updating them so they are accurate and relevant.

3. Companies use generic job descriptions that can easily be applied to many other companies or job functions.

If You Can Handle 50% of the Tasks Listed in a Job Description, Then Confidently Apply

The reality is that companies make concessions all the time when it comes to hiring. Usually it's not long after the résumés start coming in that they realize they are not likely to find a candidate who matches all of their "requirements."

In other words, after interviewing candidates, they will either accept the fact they need to teach "Stacey" the specific accounting software she is going to need, or they will need to pay "Khalid" a realistic salary (more money) based on his experience and the market conditions.

Story: I worked with a client who looked to be a perfect fit for an open position based both on her experience and the company's job description. However, she was hesitant about applying because she didn't fit the criteria of the last bullet in the company's 15-bullet-point job description. This woman was amazing and had already accomplished so much in her career; setting up sophisticated healthcare technology systems. She was also very personable and yet, here she was letting one bullet point shake her confidence about applying to the company.

Remember, this is a marketplace and the company, by posting a job, is just initiating the transaction. They may want loads of experience and knowledge at bargain basement prices but that does not mean they are going to get it.

Story: Years ago, my colleague and I were looking to hire an associate-level marketing person for our team. When the job description was sent out, it required one year of marketing experience. Our manager at the time insisted on it. We spoke with HR and told her that one year of marketing experience was not necessary as this was a lower level role and we would take on the responsibility of bringing this person up to speed. Weeks went by and when HR was not interviewing the candidates they had hoped for, they went back through the pile of over 100 résumés and started pulling out candidates who looked interesting but did not have the "minimum of one year of marketing experience."

Guess what happened? We hired a woman who learned incredibly quickly, was a pleasure to work with, and did an amazing job.

Companies need good people and good, capable people are not easy to find. If you can do 50% of what a company is "requiring," then you can apply with confidence.

Wrapping Up

Don't be shy about applying to companies with this new approach as you never know who could read your résumé. It's totally reasonable to think a manager will like your approach of mailing her your résumé and want to interview you. Furthermore, the two of you could then have a great discussion during your interview and she will be willing to train you for whatever additional skills you may need for the role. I've seen this happen over and over again.

The next chapter is all about the other avenue job seekers can go down when searching for a job; working with third-party recruiters. There is a lot to know before engaging with these professionals and I'm going to take you through all of it right now.

7

Managing Third-Party Recruiters

If you have not applied for jobs in a while, or if you are relatively new to the job market, then you need to pay close attention to this chapter.

Who Are Third-Party Recruiters?

Third-party recruiters (also known as headhunters, external recruiters, staffing or talent acquisition specialists, talent agents, among other titles) are professionals who companies hire to help them find candidates for open positions. The recruiters can either work for small or larger organizations or they can be independent contractors.

Regardless of where they work, it is important to understand that third-party recruiters work for the <u>companies they are helping</u>, not you. They have a financial interest in placing you, therefore, all of their advice to you must be taken with this in mind.

Remember in the last chapter when I said companies get flooded with résumés? Well, one of the work-arounds for companies (other than ATS) is to have these external recruiters take care of this part of the process for them, so they don't have to comb through piles of résumés. Recruiters will do the initial screening of candidates and then present companies with several options, so the process is more manageable and efficient.

There are both positives and negatives with having third-party recruiters as part of your job search. Let's discuss both.

The Positives

1. If you connect with a recruiter and he or she winds up sending your résumé to a company, then you are substantially increasing your chances of your résumé being seen and then getting called for an interview.

2. A lot of times these recruiters have established relationships with the companies they represent which also means they have a good idea of what a particular hiring manager is looking for and what types of questions you can expect during the interview. This is incredibly valuable information.

3. Recruiters will help negotiate your salary and other benefits on your behalf so you do not need to speak with the company directly about any of those topics.

Note: Chapter 9 goes into much more detail about salary negotiations and it's important that you have a handle on what you should and should not say during these discussions.

4. If you do not get an interview or an offer, and you enjoyed working with the recruiter, then you now have a new contact for possible future opportunities.

The Negatives

1. Recruiters only get paid (or earn a decent portion of their compensation) when you agree to a company's offer. In other words, they work on commission. Therefore, they may try to justify a weak dollar offer or a company's unwillingness to give you an extra week of vacation in the hopes that you'll sign your offer letter so they can get paid. Only *you* know what's really best for you.

2. Low barrier to entry. In today's world, almost anyone can be a recruiter and the market is, therefore, saturated with them. It can be a very cut-throat business when there are so many players which is why it's important to understand the potential pitfalls.

3. Some recruiters will use under-handed tactics to try and extract information from you that they can potentially use for their own purposes. More on this in a minute.

Over the years, I have heard (and personally experienced) many stories about questionable, rude, and/or unethical behavior toward job seekers by external recruiters. Recruiters who behave in this way are not worth your time. Only spend time working with the true professionals.

How to Connect with Recruiters

You can connect with recruiters in two ways: they reach out to you (usually via LinkedIn or your email) or you actively seek them out. Let's take each scenario separately.

They Reach out to You

This is common especially when your LinkedIn profile is updated. As I mentioned in Chapter 4, LinkedIn is very easy to search, therefore, don't be surprised if you hear from recruiters even if you are not actively job searching. They are looking for potential candidates who may be willing to entertain the idea of switching companies.

If you are contacted by a recruiter, first make sure they want to discuss a <u>specific</u> position and you get the job description from them in writing before sending your résumé along. The reason this is important is because there are some recruiters out there who will "fish" for professionals to add into their databases and will lie about having an open position just to get your résumé and other details.

Story: Here is an actual email exchange to illustrate what I mean:

A recruiter sent an email with a brief, generic job description for a position in a job seeker's general geographic location. The company and location were not revealed.

Job Seeker: Thank you for the email. Can you tell me who the company is and the location?

No response from the recruiter. Job Seeker follows up with another email three days later.

Recruiter: This is a semi-confidential search in that we are disclosing the company once we have had a pre-qualification discussion via phone.

Job Seeker: I understand. I'd like to learn more. When is a good time to chat?

Recruiter: Are you actively looking?

Job Seeker: I'm keeping my options open. I'm free Thursday morning. Will that work?

No response from the recruiter.

No decent recruiter is going to drag his feet when there is an interested candidate for an open position. This exchange was highly suspect from the radio silence the recruiter gave the job seeker after *the recruiter* initially reached out. Fortunately for the job seeker, no real time was wasted and the recruiter only got the fact that the job seeker was interested. It doesn't matter because that recruiter has already proven not to be worth the job seeker's time.

Look out for nonsense like this.

There are right ways to build relationships and there are many wrong ways to go about it. Just be diligent and aware like you would when someone you don't know reaches out and starts asking for sensitive information.

You Reach out to Them

If you find you are having trouble searching on your own, either because of time or other constraints, then you can proactively reach out to recruiters as they may be able to help you.

As mentioned, there are organizations that have many recruiters in house and you can call or email the company (or fill out an online form), explain who you are, and start a conversation with a professional. There are also independent recruiters who are easily found on LinkedIn.

If they're smart, they will take your call and if they're professional, they'll be honest with you regarding whether they can ultimately help you then or in the future. In these cases, you will send them your résumé so they can get a clear understanding of your background and what you're looking to do next.

Note: In either case, never hand over your résumé unless you first have their agreement, in writing, that they will not send your résumé to any company without your written permission. Any good recruiter will understand this.

What's the big deal if they send out my résumé? It can't hurt, right?

Wrong.

The reason this clarification is necessary is because there are some recruiters who will send your résumé to companies without you even knowing! The problem with this is the company receiving your résumé does not know that you did not give consent, and then *you* can potentially look bad (without you even knowing), especially if a recruiter is over the line or aggressive with the company.

Don't let someone else tarnish your reputation with unprofessionalism. Guard your résumé closely and only give it out directly to companies or recruiters whom you trust and/or are comfortable with.

Speaking with Recruiters

Once recruiters have your résumé, you will most likely have a call with them so they can learn a little more about you and what you're looking to do next. This is very common and should be an easy conversation. The initial phone call should be casual but professional and fairly brief. You should not be surprised by any questions or made to feel uncomfortable in any way.

Be cognizant of how the conversation is going. A good recruiter will want to know your work history, where you are looking to go next in your career, how far you would be willing to commute, and possibly what your salary requirements would be.

Questions to Watch out for

Unfortunately, this is not always the case. All of the below questions (among others), including the many variations, are red flags. All of these questions are meant to work against you as negotiating leverage for a company; or are just plain nosy and rude.

Do not answer any of these and, if more than one comes up during a conversation, don't continue to engage with this particular recruiter. They are not worth your time.

Note: The same goes for company employees. They should *not* be asking you these types of questions either.

- What is your current salary?

- What is your salary history?

- What is the lowest salary that you'll accept?

- Do you have a family/kids?

- Do you own a home?

- How old are you?

- What year did you graduate college?

- Where are you from originally?

While some of these questions may come across as a recruiter innocently wanting to get to know you better, the fact is that *all* of these questions are offensive and none of his business.

If you reached out to a recruiter, then you will discuss what you are looking to do next as well as whether there are any current openings that might be a potential fit. And, if you are speaking to him about a specific role, then you will talk about your work history, your salary requirements, and also work to learn as much about the new role as he can tell you. That's it.

All of those other questions are totally irrelevant and, in some cases, illegal.

Recruiters are not your career counselor, friend, or mentor. They are <u>agents for a company</u> and are trying to earn a commission by placing you. Your relationship with a recruiter is also a **business relationship**. You don't need to answer offensive questions to be seriously considered for open positions, so don't allow them to make you feel small in any way. You are in total control of these interactions.

Finally, like with many of the topics in this book, use your gut. If recruiters (or anyone else you connect with) are making any types of disparaging or negative comments about you or your work history, you don't have to tolerate it. Your work history is what it is and you have nothing to apologize for. Don't get involved with someone who doesn't take the time to understand who you are and what you are looking to do next. Do not get drawn into a bad relationship. If it doesn't feel right, walk away and cut off all communication. There are plenty of good recruiters out there with whom you can work.

Knowledge Is Power

This book, especially this chapter, is meant to empower you on your journey to your next job. The more information you have about all of these moving parts, the more powerful you will be which will quickly translate into confidence.

Confidence impacts everything we do and everyone we meet in a positive way. Having confidence in yourself is the keystone to becoming a strong and successful job seeker, and this confidence will serve you best during the most important part of the process, the interview.

8

Interview with Confidence

The next step in the job search process is the interview. So many job seekers put a tremendous amount of pressure on themselves for interviews, and rightfully so. Many interviews are conducted with you having no insights into the personalities of the people you will be meeting with or what questions you will receive. Everything about that is unnerving.

The good news is that there are simple steps you can take to put yourself at ease to help you make the most of the opportunity in front of you.

A New Mindset Is the First Part

The first and most important concept is to, again, change your mindset about the interview itself. As mentioned in Chapter 2, companies <u>need you</u> in order to function properly. And, if they want talented employees, then they need to have their act together when it comes time to interview candidates.

You Are Interviewing the Company as Much as the Company Is Interviewing You

So many candidates go into interviews with the mindset of "I hope they like me." This is a very passive and weak frame of mind that does not benefit you in any way. You need to shift your mindset to realize that you also need to like the company. Just because a company has an open position, does not mean it will be a good fit for *your* needs.

There Are Both Good and Bad Managers and Good and Bad Companies

Good managers will conduct professional interviews and be friendly. Bad managers will be rude and maybe even obnoxious. You will only be meeting someone for roughly an hour, if that. While that's not nearly enough time to really get to know someone on a deeper level, it *is* enough time to draw the conclusion that how they act during your interview will be a very good indicator of how they will treat you as an employee. And once you know this information, you can then reconcile that piece with all of the other factors to decide whether the opportunity is still worth pursuing.

Additionally, pay close attention to how the company, as a whole, treats you and your time during the entire process. Freeing up time to interview, especially if you are currently working, is not always easy and/or convenient. Companies who respect candidates will recognize that and work to make the process as efficient as possible. Bad companies will not do this.

Story: An external recruiter reached out to Roy for an associate level finance role at a company. What started out as initial interest morphed into a three-month interview process that was confusing, disorganized, and frustrating.

Roy did come across several negative, online reviews about the company but decided to pursue the opportunity anyway. Throughout the whole process, he tried to uncover why the whole finance team was new and still understaffed. He did get confirmation that many finance employees had recently quit around the same time for various reasons and yet, despite confirming some of the negative reviews, Roy ignored the initial signs and continued with the interview process.

Normally, lower level finance roles require the candidate to interview with only a few people; the most important one being the candidate's future manager. After the initial phone screen, this particular company's process started with in-person interviews with two managers and the Finance Director. Those interviews were supposed to be the only interviews, but the recruiter reached back out a week later because the company decided that he needed to have a fourth in-person interview with a Vice President. After this interview, Roy spoke with another HR representative over the phone.

Roy was finally offered the job almost three months after the initial recruiter's phone call to him. He accepted but, before he was scheduled to start his new role, the company delayed the start date for several months until the new year. When he asked the recruiter why, the recruiter's answer was "budget reasons."

Needless to say, Roy was no longer interested in this company.

Watch the Signs!

This is a great example of a company not valuing or respecting the candidate's time. This story also illustrates a candidate recognizing the initial signs but choosing to go along with this particular company's overkill interviewing process. While some companies do choose to interview more extensively than others, this was close to an entry level role. This company clearly did not trust its managers and director to make the hiring decision and, instead, involved too many people in the process.

This company also had no regard for all the time Roy needed to set aside just to be available to interview. Four rounds of interviews mean about three to four hours of time that he needed to find, including taking days off or leaving work early. This enormous inconvenience should have been the final red flag to him that this company did not value his time.

If a company does not treat you well during the interview process, then don't expect to be treated much better once you're an employee. It's really that simple.

Preparation Is the Second Part

Mindset aside, another way to give yourself confidence and reduce your nerves is to prepare.

This may seem like a no-brainer to some of you, but there are candidates out there who do not take the time to learn about a company. Demonstrating to a company that you did your homework prior to your interview will go a long way, especially if you feel like you stumbled or gave a weak answer to a question. In the end, the more prepared candidate will stand out.

If a company is public, read their recent press releases, annual reports, Corporate Social Responsibility reports, and 10-Ks to learn about the highlights as well as the main issues facing the company. These documents are typically found on a company's website, sometimes under "Investor Relations." You do not have to read these documents cover to cover (they're long and very dry) but there are sections found in the beginning that clearly illustrate many key points about the company.

Alternatively, if a company is private, read whatever information you can find on their website and social media pages as well as any articles that populate when you search for the company online.

Have a set of answers for standard interview questions, including behavioral questions[3], that you will likely be asked and continuously practice these answers out loud either to someone you trust or to yourself. Literally speak the words audibly as it usually takes a few times to work out the kinks. Don't answer these questions out loud for the first time during the interview. It will show, especially if you haven't interviewed for a while.

Note: A list of several behavioral questions can also be found in the Appendix.

Is there a good way to answer behavioral questions?

Yes. There is a method known as the S.T.A.R. method. The acronym stands for Situation, Task, Action, and Result, and is a great guide for answering any behavioral question.

---

[3] Behavioral questions typically start with "Tell me about a time when you..." or "Give me an example of when you..." These are common questions and are used by interviewers to simply help them understand how you think, work, etc.

Here's how it works. The interviewer will ask you a behavioral question, for example:

Tell me about a time you overcame a challenge?

Note: This is just one example. If you don't have an example that specifically addresses the question, chances are you have an example that's *close*. That's fine. Use that one.

To construct an answer, break down the facts into the four buckets, like this:

Situation: A manager overseeing a critical new product launch suddenly left the company. This project, the company's biggest initiative for the year, now had no one to guide the team and a lot of uncertainty surrounded the timeline.

Task: I was asked to take over the project, create a new timeline based on the state of the project, and deliver the new product to the market at the originally scheduled time.

Action: I first sent an email to everyone involved in the project, alerting them to the new circumstances. I then called the heads of all of the departments to get a handle of where they were and what they were waiting on in order to continue to move forward. Additionally, I needed my colleagues to tell me the outside vendor timelines (printers, container manufacturers, ingredient suppliers, among others) so I could understand what constraints I was under. Finally, I personally spoke with the packaging designer to understand where the project was left off and when decisions needed to be made by.

Result: After developing a new timeline, obtaining final signoff on the packaging and the product itself, I kept the project on track and led the team to successfully deliver the new product on time.

Note: When delivering the answer don't use the words "situation," "task," "action," and "result." You don't need to. Use those words only as a guide when constructing your answers ahead of time.

Note 2: The S.T.A.R. format is for behavioral questions only. If you are asked specifically about a project or deliverable, just respond in a regular way like you would in any conversation.

If you take the time to practice answering these questions on your own at home (out loud) in this format, these answers will come out clear and polished, giving you a leg up on many other candidates.

Know Your Work History

Familiarize yourself with all the bullet points on your résumé as well as other stories and achievements from your past. The best way to do this is to write down anything you can remember from old jobs so they are more in the forefront of your memory. You may get a question where the best response involves a story that is not on your résumé. That's okay, as long as you can quickly call it up. If you try and recall old examples during an interview, it will likely be very difficult to do while you're under pressure and could make you nervous and shake your confidence. Take the time <u>now</u> to revisit those old work stories so you can easily speak to them if necessary.

Changing your mindset by recognizing that you and the company are both looking for a good fit, taking the time to learn about a company, practicing answers to common questions, and reviewing your résumé, will allow you to relax, be confident, and enjoy the interview process.

Three Types of Interviews

We are now going to breakdown three main types of interviews individually, some common questions you will likely receive, and questions you need to be ready to ask the company.

Phone Interviews

Phone interviews are very common and are typically used by a company as an initial screening process. They can last anywhere from 20-60 minutes and are designed so HR can get to know you as well as tell you more about the company and the role. In the end though, the call is primarily used to determine if you are a candidate they want to move ahead with in the hiring process.

Note: Every company is different. In some cases, the hiring manager will conduct the first phone screen and not HR. Regardless of how a company handles its interviewing process, the insights in this chapter will apply to all cases.

The positives are that phone interviews are convenient, short, and comfortable. They also give you a chance to learn about the company before deciding to commit any further time if you're not happy with how the call went and/or what you learned about the company and the position. In addition, you don't have to memorize quite as much as you can keep notes and other materials nearby while you're on the phone.

Caution: Don't rely on your notes too heavily as it will be obvious if you're rifling through papers to help you answer questions.

The negative side is that you have to project your personality and enthusiasm *entirely* through your voice. In other words, if you talk a lot with your hands and make good eye contact, none of that will directly help you over the phone. Therefore, you need to speak up and make sure you inflect your voice and not speak in a monotone. Find the balance between the voice you would use to talk to a friend while also being polite and professional. Remember, this is the company's very first direct contact with you, so you want to make a great impression!

Some questions that you must anticipate for these initial calls include:

1. Tell me a little about yourself? -or- Why don't you take me through your résumé?

Note: Both of these questions are asking the same thing. This is where you do your résumé walk. They are not asking you to divulge your personal information or your autobiography. Always keep these interactions professional. An example of a résumé walk is later in this chapter.

2. What interests you about this role and our company?

3. Why are you looking to leave your current role?

4. What are you looking for in terms of compensation?

5. What is your current salary?*

Note: <u>Never</u> answer this question. Answer the above question (#4), instead. We'll get much more into this topic in the next chapter.

6. Do you have any questions for me?

Make sure you have some thoughtful questions for the interviewer. If you are speaking with HR, she may not have the best answers about the specific role, so you can gear these initial questions to be more about the company itself and the culture.

Some examples could include:

1. Is this a new position? If not, is the role open because someone left or was promoted?

2. What do you enjoy most about working at this company?

3. Can you give me an example or two that illustrates the company culture?

Notice how I didn't ask, "What is the company culture like?" That question opens the door to a canned answer that goes something like: "It's a team atmosphere ... very collaborative ... etc."

Instead, ask for a specific example or two to get the real answer. If she cannot come up with good examples, then make a note to ask someone else later on to see if there really is anything special (or not) about the company's culture.

Note: Do not bring up vacation time, benefits, or salary unless the company brings it up first. Save those details for after the in-person interview(s).

Clarify what the next steps are so you know when to expect to hear back from the company.

Video Interviews

These have become more popular as video calls are free and easy. There are positives and negatives with these as well which we will go through now.

The positive is that you and the employer can have a more natural conversation and take facial queues from each other. Your smile and enthusiasm will show much more easily.

The negative is that if the internet or phone connection is bad or gets interrupted, it could be tricky to hear or be heard, which could disrupt the conversation. Video calls are also not as convenient as regular phone interviews as you will need to be home for it (most likely) and dress the part (business formal) even though you're not meeting in person.

Additionally, a quirk with video chats is that there is a tendency to look at the other person's *face* on your screen. The problem with that is when they are looking back at you, your eyes are not on them. Therefore, you need to force yourself to look at <u>your camera</u> both when you are speaking as well as when you are listening, so it appears as if you're making eye contact. If you do this and also catch periodic glances at the person's face on the screen, you'll be fine. It's an easy adjustment to make and the interaction will come across as more natural.

Prior to the call, set up your screen so your face is centered and the bottom of the screen is just past your shoulders. Make sure the lighting is good. Usually natural light and/or a desk lamp is sufficient. Also, ensure your background (usually the wall behind you) is not distracting or messy. The point is to be fully ready to go when the interview starts so you're not scrambling at the last minute or taking time out of the interview to get set up.

Once the initial phone screen is done, or if a video call was done in place of an initial phone interview, it is very possible that you will have a second round of interviews either via phone or video. Again, every company is different and the same steps listed above will still apply, with the following exceptions:

The next round of calls will most likely be longer and more involved and you will need to have those other questions ready that you could not ask HR about. These are your more meaningful questions about the role, the team, and what you'll be working on.

A few examples of questions to your potential manager could be:

1. How will I be interacting with you and the group?

2. What are your expectations of me and your measures of success for this role?

3. **A business question.** This question should focus specifically on the company to show you did your research. While the interviewer may not be able, or willing, to get into specifics, this question will still go a long way in terms of showing her you have taken the time to research and think about the company and the role.

One-Way Video

Some companies are now using one-way video interviews where candidates are given questions on a screen and have a few, timed minutes to answer them. Keep in mind, you are not actually speaking with anyone, rather the company is recording your video answers so several employees can later watch your recorded answers and then discuss whether to bring you in for a next round of interviews.

Needless to say, this is very unnatural so just do your best. Look at the camera, smile, and use whatever time you need (up to the limit) to answer the questions. It's just a screening process that takes about 20 to 30 minutes.

In-Person Interviews

This is the big one. This is where you want to be in the process. This is where the final decision is made by the company regarding whether they want to extend you an offer and where *you* will make your final decision about whether you're still interested in the opportunity.

The Basics

1. Dress – Business formal (suits) unless otherwise clearly stated. If you're not sure, wear a suit. It's better to be overdressed than underdressed.

Note: I've read that some start-up companies take exception if candidates show up in suits since their work culture is typically more casual. Easy fix. For those of you interviewing with start-up companies, just ask the question prior to showing up. If they tell you to wear what you want, don't wear a suit, but dress neatly; business casual as a general guide.

2. Know *exactly* where you are going – With GPS, it's almost impossible to get lost but, honestly, make sure you know where the office is located and how long it will take you to get there. Also, be sure there are convenient alternate routes that make sense to you.

Story: Years ago, I had an interview at a large corporate park. There were four main buildings but they were spread out. I could not see the numbers on the buildings anywhere and it was raining. Thankfully, I was early, as I managed to park my car and go into the wrong building, twice. Needless to say, this added a layer of stress I really didn't need before meeting with two vice-presidents and two directors.

3. Leave plenty of time – Don't cut it close. Car accidents happen. Trains breakdown. Sometimes it hails for no reason. Get to where you need to be *at least* a half hour early. Don't check in, just sit in your car or find a nearby coffee shop if you're in a big city. Be respectful of the company's time, too. If your interview is at 10:00 a.m., check in with security or a receptionist at 9:50 a.m. You may still need to wait a few minutes. That's fine. You're on time, not annoyingly early.

4. Carry a pen, three to four copies of your résumé (regular, white paper is fine), and a padfolio – You can get inexpensive padfolios online for about ten bucks. You probably won't ever use it for anything else, so don't buy an expensive one. It's also good to carry some breath mints (the ones that don't rattle) and a few tissues in case of a rogue sneeze or a runny nose.

5. Turn your phone OFF – Don't just put it on vibrate, turn it off.

6. Seriously, O-F-F

7. Firm handshake and eye contact – First impressions say a lot. You don't need to make a vice grip handshake, just make sure it's firm. If you're unsure, practice with some friends. It will take no time at all. Then, when it's time to meet your interviewers, you can look them directly in the eye, shake their hand with confidence and…

8. Smile! – You're not being held against your will. You're discussing your background and learning about what could potentially be a great step forward in your career. This is exciting!

Game Time

Let's now move on to the actual interview and what to look out for, how to control your nerves, as well as what to do and what not to do.

This is where you, as a newly minted, hyper-aware, pro-active job seeker, will start to use your senses to pay very close attention to how the remainder of the process goes.

You'll be having a series of conversations and, more likely than not, your gut will tell you how you feel when it's all over. So just relax and get ready to have a chat with some nice folks.

You will most likely be shown into a room where you will either stay for the duration of your visit or for the first one or two interviews. Alternatively, you may sit in someone's office. Just be open and ready for anything.

If the person who showed you into the room asks if you want anything, ask for water. You will be doing a lot of talking and your mouth will get dry. Many companies will likely offer you water when you show up. Take it. You'll need it.

They're Excited to Meet You. Be Excited to Meet Them!

Remember, you were *invited* to interview, not summoned! They obviously saw something in both your résumé and the initial phone screen that indicated to them that you could potentially be a great fit for their organization.

Common Questions

Regardless of the industry you're in, the majority of job seekers are going to get a set of similar questions followed by industry or role specific questions.

More often than not, interviewers like to ask the following question right out of the gate:

Can you walk me through your résumé?

This question is a gift. You can (and will) have this answer ready to go because you will have rehearsed it ahead of time; many, many times. The best way to answer this is to hit on the jobs that are most relevant (if you've been working a long time) or all of the jobs if you've been working roughly 15 years or less. These jobs will be the ones on your résumé that the interviewer will have in front of her. She will probably follow along on the page while you are speaking.

The key to this answer is to tell a *story*. An interesting take on where you worked, an accomplishment or things you learned, why you changed jobs, and where you are now…all the way up to the interview you're currently having. Keep your response, if you were to say it all the way through without interruption, to about 3-4 minutes. The interviewer may interrupt you to ask questions about certain roles. No problem! You know your prior experience better than anyone and since you prepared this response ahead of time, these questions will be manageable and you'll be able to pick up your story exactly where you left off.

Here is an example of a résumé walk. When you deliver your own résumé walk, be sure to infuse your personality into it and make it conversational.

I graduated from Ohio University with a degree in economics and started working at ABC Corporation as a Customer Account Specialist. This was really a great first role as it taught me so much including fundamental business knowledge, solid communication skills, and customer service practices that still serve me well today.

After about a year and a half, I transitioned to a Marketing Specialist position based on my interest in the field and the good work that I did in Customer Accounts. The communication skills I learned in my first position really enabled me to work well with our sales force and other internal groups to develop and execute various marketing programs. I also gained budget and vendor management responsibilities in this role, which was new for me. I carefully helped manage our budget to efficiently spend our limited dollars on meaningful programs that helped elevate the brand.

After almost four years at ABC, I accepted an offer from XYZ Industries as a Brand Manager for their Top-Line brand. In this role, I had full responsibility to develop and execute several new product launches that were key to the brand and the company's overall strategic vision. I was also responsible for analyzing our sales data and presenting monthly updates to senior leaders along with working on and participating in bi-annual sales meetings to formally present the latest marketing initiatives to our sales team.

It's been a great three years at XYZ as I've really been able to round out my skillset and move my career along in marketing. This position at Corporation of America interests me as it would be a step up in responsibility while having the ability to help set the strategy and manage a business for products that I really love.

You don't need to (nor should you) cover everything during your résumé walk. Keep it pretty high level as you want to hold the interviewer's interest and not bore her with tons of details. If she is interested in knowing more about a certain role or project, she will either stop you during your résumé walk or ask you at the end. This is where you can go into more detail to effectively answer her questions.

In general, like you would with any conversation, pay attention to your audience. If you feel you are losing them with your answers, make sure you're not speaking in a monotone or dragging your answers out too long. You're going to know this and many other rehearsed answers cold. Deliver them with enthusiasm!

Story: One of the most interesting interview questions related to this was when an interviewer asked me to give him my résumé walk in <u>one minute</u>. Talk about boiling it down to the highlights of the highlights! Give it a try. It's good to have the ability to speak to your experience in very short bursts as well as for extended periods.

Now, the question that usually follows your résumé walk is:

What are you looking to do now? and/or *Why are you interested in our company?*

Again, easy – because you know it's coming and you have your thoughtful answer prepared and rehearsed. You can either tack it on to the end of your résumé walk, like in my example, or wait for them to ask. Either is fine.

Job Seeker Concerns

What if I got laid off or quit my last job? If I'm not working at the moment, that's certainly going to come up.

You tell the truth. Companies have layoffs all the time and even great employees are not immune to companies' budget cuts or reorganizations. It's nothing to be ashamed of. If you attempt to lie or muddle your story and the company does a background check, then your lie could potentially be exposed and you could eliminate your chances of moving forward with this new company, not to mention tarnish your reputation.

If you quit your previous job and are currently unemployed, then you say, "It was time to move on and find a new challenge and I was more comfortable job searching full-time."

Won't some people be skeptical of that answer?

Some will, sure, but it doesn't matter. If they are focusing on why you left a company (which you are entitled to do, by the way) instead of focusing on the fact that you are available to start working for their company very quickly, then they are missing a valuable opportunity.

This is a great example of where that old school advice and this advice differ completely.

The old school mentality is that your chances of landing a job are diminished if you're not currently working as your potential future employer will think there is something wrong with you.

First of all, who's to say what anyone is thinking? Remember the good managers and bad managers? Bad managers focus on that type of stuff and good ones focus on opportunities and finding the right people because as I said earlier, finding good people is not easy.

My advice is to project confidence that you are in complete control of your situation, because you are! Whether you quit a previous job or the company decided to eliminate your position, you are excited and ready to find your next challenge.

Tip: If you are unemployed but have an opportunity to help a company or a friend, even if it's for free, then you tell people you are a consultant while you're searching for your next opportunity. Add it to your résumé, as well.

What if the company asks a lot of terrible questions?

That's certainly possible. No one likes to receive worthless questions like *"What's your biggest weakness?"* or *"Why are you the best candidate for this job?"* Keep in mind that these questions make the interviewer look bad, not you. These are the types of questions interviewers fall back on when they didn't take the time to really read your résumé, don't have a lot of experience interviewing candidates, or are simply poor interviewers.

As I mentioned in the beginning of this chapter, you don't know what questions you are going to get, so don't sweat it. If they are asking you these questions, then they are also asking other candidates the same questions. Keep your answers positive, smile, and try to quickly move on to the next question.

Note: Don't be afraid to ask interviewers if you can ask a question about the role to break a potential, rigid question and answer session. If you can get your interviewer to have more of a conversation with you, then the interview will be so much more natural and relaxed.

Remember, these interviews are *discussions*, not interrogations! In the absolute worst of cases, you can always leave the interview. Hopefully this does not happen but, if, for some reason the interview becomes contentious or you feel uncomfortable because of a string of unprofessional questions, then you can always get up, say thank you, and walk right out the front door. You <u>never</u> have to sit through any situation that is unprofessional or unwelcoming. Sure, an interviewer may throw some tough, thought provoking questions at you, but as long as they are work-related and not uncomfortably personal, that's fine. You'll be ready.

Bring Good Questions with You

A good interviewer will allow plenty of time for you to ask questions, ideally not just at the very end. Exactly when you can ask your questions may not be in your control but what *is* in your control are the actual questions you ask. This is another area where you can really stand out from other candidates.

During your interview preparation, come up with five or six *specific* questions about the company and write them down inside your padfolio. There is no need to memorize these questions. In fact, you may come up with some new questions during your interview that are even better than what you originally planned to ask. If that happens, jot them down and ask the best ones first.

Story: Years ago, I was interviewing at a food company and one of the topics that came up during the discussion was distribution. When I had a chance to ask questions, I mentioned that particular point from earlier and asked why the company didn't have distribution in the big club stores and if there were any plans to do so.

"Great question," she said, and then proceeded to give me a very interesting answer about the company's overall club store strategy.

It was a good question because it was specific to the role and showed I was thinking about the company and the business in a meaningful way, not to mention listening to what she had said earlier in the conversation. If I had, instead, led with, "Tell me about a typical day here," it would not have been nearly as impactful.

When do I bring up the work hours and any travel?

Both of these topics should really be initiated by the company at some point in the process, however, that's not always the case. Let's take these two separately.

Travel – Many job descriptions list the percentage of travel, although not always. Certain roles lend themselves to more travel (i.c. sales) while others do not. If you're interviewing for a role that does not normally include a lot of travel, ask the question during your interview with your potential manager. Make sure you understand how much travel there will be (i.e. how many days or weeks per year) and where you would potentially go.

Don't make it your first question, save it for the end of the interview. It's a fair question but, as I mentioned earlier, ask the more thoughtful questions first. If you don't get to ask this question, just make sure you get the answer before signing an offer letter.

Work hours – This one is a little more sensitive as asking about work hours too early doesn't always sit well with people. If no one brings up the subject during all of the interviews you have, wait until you have your offer letter. At that point, reach out to the hiring manager directly, even if you're working with a third-party recruiter, and ask for ten minutes as you have a couple of more questions.

Wrapping Up

Ask everyone you interview with for their business card so you have their contact information. If they don't have a business card for you (or if you just had a phone or video interview), ask for their email address. They'll know why you want it and should not hesitate to give it to you. Before you leave the interview, make sure you have a clear understanding of what the next steps are and when you should expect to hear back from the company. You will likely hear from HR, unless you are working with a third-party recruiter.

Thank You Notes After Each Interview

Send a thank you note, via email, either later that night or first thing the next morning to *each* person you interviewed with. They took time out of their day to get to know you. Thank them individually for doing so.

Note: Be sure to send thank you notes after every phone and video interview as well.

Keep these emails really brief and upbeat. Here's an example:

Dear Carmela,

I just wanted to take a moment to thank you for your time during my interview yesterday. I really enjoyed our conversation and I appreciate you sharing some of the exciting future plans in store for the company. I look forward to learning more. Have a great day.

Regards,
Tony

Four sentences that thank the interviewer and mention one particular detail that stood out to you. "I look forward to learning more" is a more finessed way of saying "I really want to be considered for this job." Your note can be written clearly and professionally at the same time.

Note: It's been my experience that most people do not respond to thank you notes. Even though you may not get a response, these notes will still go a long way as many interviewers have come to expect them.

Following Up

Be proactive with this part of the job search process as well. It's not over yet.

If you are working with a third-party recruiter, he will be excited to know how the interview went. In fact, he will probably expect you to call him immediately. You don't have to contact him immediately. Digest your whole interview experience internally, or with family and friends, and then get back to him either later that day or the next morning.

Feel free to share with him what you learned and your thoughts, but play it cool. Never forget that third-party recruiters are still on the company's side of this negotiation, not yours, so you want to be level-headed about your feedback.

If you are not working with a third-party recruiter, mark your calendar for one-week from the interview and follow up with the HR representative (or the proper contact) if you have not heard anything.

In either case, do not wait around for them. Continue to job search and send out letters. Your time is valuable when you are job searching. Don't let a week go by because you thought the interview went well and sense an offer on the horizon. Hopefully a good offer *is* on the horizon, but it's important to note that things can change in companies very quickly. I've seen open positions close because of budget cuts and other reasons that have nothing to do with you.

I'm really sick of not hearing anything from companies after I interview with them.

This is, by far, the biggest unprofessional infraction that many companies do. "Ghosting" candidates, or leaving them hanging forever, is an inexcusable practice that happens way too frequently. I cannot figure out why anyone inside a company does not realize the damage they are causing to their own image by doing this.

Here is a quick story of how companies "ghost" candidates if you are unfamiliar with this practice.

Story: I had a friend who interviewed at an established, well-known company a couple of years ago and this exact thing happened to him. He went back twice for in-person interviews and the company never got back to him and his third-party recruiter, even after many repeated requests for an update. This friend was all but certain that the job was his and while it would have been disappointing to get a rejection, it was *far worse* getting no response at all. It's demoralizing, deflating, and completely unprofessional to be treated that way by anyone, let alone an organization trying to fill a role.

What that particular company missed (and others are missing) is they didn't merely turn him off from ever considering them again, but they have also turned anyone else off who heard about this behavior. Think about it, why would anyone commit to exploring an opportunity with a company they know treated their friend so poorly?

Just because ghosting is a relatively common practice, does not mean it's okay or professional.

The only way to combat this nonsense is to do what I've already said:

Move on. Do not wait on anyone or any company. Keep pressing on with exploring new opportunities, connecting with people, mailing out cover letters and résumés, and having interviews. This pro-active approach will disable any "hold" a company may have on you by keeping you waiting.

It's so simple but very empowering.

Note: More recently, there have been stories of candidates ghosting companies. Please, don't do this. You are not required to continue with any interview or accept any offer you do not wish to pursue. Additionally, you do not need to give a reason for changing your mind, even though the company will be curious. Instead, do the professionally courteous thing, regardless of where you are in the process, and let your contact at the company know that you would no longer like to be considered for the job opportunity. A brief email or phone call takes only a few minutes and is the right way to handle this situation.

Two Final Interview Stories

As I mentioned several times already, the signs are everywhere. Here are two more stories that illustrate what it means to look out for the signs during interviews. The first story is about two phone interviews and the second is about an in-person interview.

Story 1: Kevin had recently left a company without having another job waiting for him. The reason he left was because the previous company had become so toxic and was negatively impacting him mentally and physically. He discussed it with his wife and decided he would prefer to spend his time job searching full-time rather than remain miserable every day at a company that didn't value his efforts or care about helping him succeed.

The first phone interview he had was with HR. The call went well enough until she asked Kevin about why he left his last company after only one year. Knowing he couldn't badmouth the company, he stated that it was no longer a good fit. The HR representative continually asked him about his former company to the point where Kevin kept repeating himself.

He was invited to a second interview, this time with the hiring manager, over the phone. Ten minutes into the phone call, he received the same treatment from the hiring manager about leaving his current position as he did from the HR person. After giving his reasons again, the hiring manager proceeded to then offer unsolicited "coaching" about why leaving a company after only a year is not a good idea. After her condescending rant was over,

Kevin politely thanked her for her time, explained that the position was no longer the right fit for him, and hung up the phone.

Kevin knew ten minutes into that second phone interview that this particular company was not worth his time because the hiring manager (his future boss) was unprofessional and obnoxious.

Kevin's a nice guy. He didn't go in looking for an argument. He was patient and professional, even after HR's borderline interrogation. Those two employees gave Kevin a clear sign: Stay away from this company! So, he did.

I'm happy to report that Kevin is now working at a great company where there was no condescending, not-asked-for coaching during the interview process because the company is a professional organization with quality employees.

Story 2: Jordan had been actively looking for a marketing role for several months. He was in his mid-20s, living at home, and had little confidence. He was beyond frustrated with not hearing back from companies even though he knew he was a great fit for many job openings based on the descriptions and his background.

An opportunity came through a "placement agency." The opportunity was not directly what he was looking for, but he thought it could be a worthwhile temporary position while he continued to look for something more permanent. He showed up at the agency and spoke with a representative there. This person told him about a temporary position at a company that paid hourly. He filled out some forms including a W-4.

The placement agency then set up an interview for him at the company for one morning at 11 a.m. Jordan showed up early in his suit, fully prepared to meet with the three different employees. He was seated in a conference room and he waited.

15 minutes later, the first person showed up to conduct a 30-minute interview and was distracted by her phone ringing at least twice. The other two employees were also interrupted while they were conducting their interviews and one even said to Jordan at one point, "It's a little chaotic here."

Jordan left the interview and knew there was something strange about the company. In addition to the unprofessionalism of the interviewers, the atmosphere in the office was crazy with people running around, looking harried and stressed out. He could hear employees complaining about other people as he walked through the office and he didn't have a good overall feeling about the company.

A few days later, the company made him an offer and he wound up taking the job. After accepting, he realized he would be paid by the placement agency and not the company. This point was never made clear to him either from the initial conversation with the placement agency (the W-4 form was also new to him and he didn't ask about it) or with the company.

Perhaps unsurprisingly, the experience was a total disaster. What he heard during his interview was accurate. Employees bad mouthed other employees, meetings went right through lunch, and Jordan's head spun the whole time. He quickly realized that while the position was only ever meant to be short-term, he was not going to learn anything valuable to help propel his career forward in this negative environment.

He lasted six weeks before quitting.

There are several things in this story that will serve as important learning experiences for you so you don't make the mistake of accepting and working at a position where all the initial signs are telling you not to work there.

1. The placement agency – This was a gray area as they did not make it clear to Jordan that he would be paid by them. While there is nothing wrong with that arrangement, it's a professional courtesy to make information like that clear from the beginning, especially to a younger employee.

Note: *Never* sign anything if you're unsure. Jordan could have easily taken whatever contract or forms he was given home with him to read over before signing. There was no rush to sign his name to anything.

2. The interview – This company failed miserably. At a minimum, all three interviewers should have left their phones at their desks during their interviews. It was incredibly disrespectful and unnecessary for the interview to be interrupted numerous times by ringing phones. If the interviewers were *that* busy where they couldn't even interview someone for 30 minutes, then either the company was out of control or they were.

One of the interviewers literally said, "It's a little chaotic here." Folks, comments like that are gold. It's a peek behind the curtain to what is *actually* going on at a company. Don't ignore those clues just because they have an open position. After all, maybe the reason they have an open position in the first place is because the person who used to occupy the open role left because of all the chaos!

3. He walked away – Things were so bad in those six weeks he dreaded going to work by Friday of the first week. His stomach hurt every morning and he saw no upside. Moreover, the work he was doing there was not going to help him for what he ultimately wanted to do in the future.

While you may be faced with taking a temporary job to bring in income, just ensure you don't give up looking for a better position. Also, know what you're getting into. Jordan didn't fully understand the role, but took it anyway out of desperation, and it didn't work out. Thankfully, he didn't lose anything, but did gain a valuable lesson, which was: it's not worth taking any job just to have a job if the company is a mess.

If you settle for taking anything, then it likely won't be long until you are more stressed out than you were before and possibly unhappier because you now have less time to seek out a good position.

Not Every Open Position Is Right for You

You will see signs every time you interview or communicate with someone from an organization. I'm not suggesting you make snap judgments; rather, take mental notes and then, after the whole process is over, determine if the company is right for your needs.

Job searching is a long process and the interviews are a critical step. Use the invitation to interview as an opportunity to fully assess if you will be better off in this new company versus your current situation, whatever "better" means to you. It's your career and your life and you are allowed to find the best fit for your personal and professional needs.

This was a long, but very important, chapter. The next one is all about salary negotiations and is the last piece before you sign your offer letter.

9

Effectively Negotiate Your Salary

Believe it or not, salary negotiations begin immediately upon finding a position that interests you. One of the very first pieces of information you will notice is whether a company posts a salary range within their job description. Similarly, if a recruiter contacts you, he will either provide you with that information, or not, regardless of whether he is in possession of that information.

In either scenario, it is very important to understand that all legitimate open jobs at companies have pre-determined budgets tied to them. In other words, companies already know what they are willing to pay candidates for every new position. As I mentioned earlier in the book, employees are a large and important expense at a company and these dollar amounts are carefully discussed and approved before any job is posted.

Unfortunately, the majority of job descriptions do not contain the salary range and, while I wish it was a requirement to do so, companies have the right to keep this information hidden. However, this does *not* mean they also have the upper hand when it comes to negotiating the salary for the position.

That's why this chapter is so important. Even without knowing the salary, you are no longer at a disadvantage when it comes to negotiating a fair and reasonable compensation package for yourself.

Note: Every interaction you have will be unique. Some companies will start the salary discussion on the first interview while some will wait until later in the process. As a general rule, do not agree to a second, in-person interview until you have established the salary you are seeking is in-line with what the company is willing to pay. There is no point in going any further before knowing the new position will make sense for you financially.

The Question You Will No Longer Directly Answer

The way salary discussions used to work (and sadly, still do, in many cases) was job seekers began the negotiations by answering the following question from either recruiters or HR:

What is your current salary? -or- What were you making at your previous role?

Over time, this question has become so commonplace that very few job seekers question its relevance and, instead, willingly give up their personal information. The problem is that companies then take this information and use it as a starting point for what they are going to offer you.

Note: Some companies even have the audacity to request your old W-2 tax forms. *Never* hand these documents over.

As an example, let's assume a company has internally budgeted a hypothetical new job at $90K/year (and is not including a salary range in their job description) and you are currently making $75K. Additionally, this new position is absolutely the next logical step up for you from your current position.

Guess what's likely to happen if you divulge your current salary?

The company is going to offer you a little over what you are currently making (say $80K) so you get a salary increase but they save money.

But, isn't that fair?

No, that is not fair. The company/job seeker dynamic is a marketplace. There are buyers (companies) and there are sellers (job seekers) and the price is determined by supply and demand among other factors.

If a company is looking for a "Department Manager," for example, then, based on many market factors, which we'll discuss in a moment, there is a salary range that makes sense for that position.

A candidate's previous salary is <u>not</u> one of those factors.

As an exaggerated, but relevant, example to illustrate this point, imagine you bought a home 20 years ago for $200,000. In the present day, you know the house is now worth roughly $400,000 and you're looking to sell. What if a potential buyer offered you $225,000 since it's more than you paid? What would you do? You would tell them your home is worth about $400,000 based on the market and they need to get serious with their offer.

The exact same thing applies to your job salary.

Your current and past salaries are totally irrelevant for future positions.

The good news is that times are changing and diligent job seekers (like you) know that any personal salary questions asked of you from this point forward are *off-limits* and you will not answer them ever again.

In fact, these questions are now <u>illegal</u> in several locations (including Massachusetts, New York, California, Connecticut, among many other states and cities)[4] and rightfully so. It's no one's business to know what your salary is except for you, your company, your accountant (if you have one), and anyone else with whom you choose to share your information. That's it. You wouldn't share this information with strangers. Don't share it with recruiters or companies.

Your New Approach

You will, instead, provide your salary range for a position based on your research of the position and your current situation. We will cover the research steps in a moment.

First, here is a conversation, based on an actual, initial phone discussion with a third-party recruiter, that best illustrates how to implement this approach. Keep in mind this discussion can be used with anyone, not only recruiters.

Story: In this example, a third-party recruiter initially posted a job title and a general, two sentence description of an open position online. Other topics were discussed during the call and then the salary topic came up.

---

[4] https://www.hrdive.com/news/salary-history-ban-states-list/516662/

Recruiter: So, what is your current compensation package?

Job Seeker: I'm happy to provide my salary range for this position once you send me the description and we discuss the role in more detail.

Recruiter: I will, but I need to understand what you're making now.

Job Seeker: I'm sorry but I'm not comfortable discussing that information.

Recruiter: [*Silence*] Can you, at least, give me an estimate? I just need it for a basis.

Job Seeker: No, but I can give you a range of what I'm looking for once I know more about the role.

Recruiter: Okay. I ask everyone this question, but let's move on. What else do you need to know?

There are a couple of things to mention about this conversation that are very telling in only a few sentences.

1. She "needs" to understand what the Job Seeker is making now. Alternatively, you may get "the *company* needs to know..."

This is total nonsense.

They don't *need* to know that information. They *want* that information as it gives them tremendous leverage when it comes to negotiating your salary.

2. An estimate for a "basis."

She's asking for your salary in a softer way. Don't fall for it. She wants a starting point to peg your next salary to. The salary that you are currently making in a <u>different</u> role at a <u>different</u> company has *nothing* to do with the role you are seeking and is, therefore, not a "basis" for anything.

What if a company or a recruiter says we can't continue the conversation without my current salary?

Then count your blessings they gave you a clear sign of what life is like at that company. If they don't value your financial privacy and don't think paying you a fair wage is important, then you don't need to work there. I can pretty much guarantee other aspects of that company are broken as well. Move on and forget them.

A recruiter once told me my current salary will be revealed during a background check. Is this true?

Two things here:

1. Your former company is only supposed to confirm your employment dates and the job titles you held. That's it. Your annual reviews and any other personal information should not be shared outside of the company. However, not everything is always in our control which is why…

2. It doesn't matter. You have every right to be paid fairly and if the new company finds out you're getting a big "raise" with the salary you are asking for, then good for them. Again, if they are not willing to pay you fairly, then you don't need to work there. That kind of behavior is a strong sign about how a company operates. If they can't treat you well during the interview process, then there is a good chance there will be other issues once you're on board. Watch the signs!

Do the Research

When you first come across a job description, as mentioned, a salary range will either be listed or not.

Note: Some job listings may say something along the lines of "salary commensurate with experience." If you see language like that, it's the same as if the salary is not posted. That company doesn't want to tip their hand to job seekers and this, as you now know, doesn't matter.

If a salary is posted within the job description, all you need to do is ensure the range is in line with what you are seeking. Keep in mind that you must read the job description carefully to understand as much as you can about the role, including the location, before determining if the salary range posted is reasonable and meets your needs.

If there is no salary posted, then you will still apply and/or send in your résumé and a cover letter. Just realize that you'll need to take the steps I'm about to outline <u>before</u> you speak with anyone at the company. You need to be prepared to tell them exactly what you are looking for in terms of compensation.

There is so much valuable (and free) information available, including relevant salary details, that will allow you to come to the negotiating table prepared and ready to discuss a mutually agreeable salary range and eventual offer.

Start with helpful websites like Glassdoor, LinkedIn, and Salary.com. All three of those sites, among other insights, have a lot of information to help you get an understanding of what a typical salary range is for the position you are seeking in the relevant location.

Now, while you already know the salary range for the specific position you are considering will not be listed, you can easily find similar roles at similar companies in similar geographical areas.

This is the same thing home sellers do when assessing how high to list their house on the market. They look at the "comps"—comparable homes in the area. You're doing that here utilizing the job titles, job descriptions, and location. You will want to get five or six different salaries so you can confidently provide the company with a reasonable salary range.

Note: Geography is really important, especially if you're looking to relocate. Jobs in and around New York City or other major cities will typically pay more than smaller towns for similar roles simply because it costs you more to live and/or work in or around those large cities.

What to Look For

1. Job title – Job titles are not standard and will vary among companies. Understand the alternate names for the job title you are interested in and search those previously mentioned websites for all of the variations.

2. Job responsibilities – Pay close attention to what your responsibilities will be versus what you are currently doing to confirm this new role is a step-up to more responsibilities (if that's what you're looking for) or not (if that's not what you're looking for). Additionally, make sure the position is something you *want* to do. Don't forget to also know how much travel will be required for the role.

3. Geographic location – Is the position in or near a big city, a small city, or a more suburban area? What will your commute be like? What will your commute cost in terms of time and money?

4. Benefits – This includes health insurance, 401(k), vacation time, and other perks.

Note: You may not have all of the benefits information at first. That's okay. Assume there are benefits and if you find out different information later on, you can adjust your range. Companies need to be transparent with this information during the interview process and if they are not, you can certainly adjust your figures to meet your needs as well (i.e. a higher base salary if no health benefits are offered).

5. Alternative to your current situation / Intangibles – Maybe you are currently unhappy at your job or maybe you're unemployed. Those two situations will impact you differently than if you are happily employed, casually exploring other potential opportunities out there. After you have all of the information (post-interviews), the last piece that goes into your decision has to do with all of the other factors that are unique to your life and current situation. We'll cover this topic later in the chapter.

Pretty straightforward, right? The key is to take the extra time to dig into job descriptions a little more by utilizing available information so you come to the negotiation table fully prepared.

Next Step

Okay, so let's say you have established your desired salary range of $90-$95K works for the company and they also want to make you an offer.

If you're working with a third-party recruiter, you and she will typically hash out the details verbally and then the company will present you with a formal offer letter. If you're working directly with the company, the verbal back and forth may or may not happen and you may just be presented with a letter. Either way is fine. The offer letter is what counts.

The offer letter is where all of the details for your new position need to be stated. This includes, but is not limited to:

- Job title

- Start date

- Base salary

- Bonus potential

- Vacation time

- Name of your direct manager

- Benefits (health insurance, 401(k), etc.)

Note: There is typically a lot of legal language included with offer letters. Read it all very carefully and make sure you understand everything _before_ you sign. If you have questions, contact the company and speak with someone until all of your questions are answered.

Wrapping Up

Receiving an offer is a great accomplishment and one that you should feel proud of. Let's take one last scenario and story to bring this chapter to a close.

If we continue with our previous example, let's say you receive an offer letter which states a base salary of $90K, three weeks' vacation, 15% potential bonus to be paid at the end of the year, full benefits, and reporting to Rob.

You have a choice here. The base salary is at the low end of your range, but you really liked Rob during your interview and you're excited that he will be your manager. The vacation time, which is actually a week more than you currently have, is secretly more important to you than any potential base salary increase the company may be willing to make. The rest of the terms are as expected.

Should I mention the lower salary?

Yes, absolutely.

All of the cards are now on the table. You schedule a time to speak with HR (or your recruiter) about your initial discussion of a base salary between $90-$95K to see if they are willing to meet you in the middle. They obviously like you and want you to come work for them but you don't need to sacrifice money simply because their initial offer is low. They are free to offer you whatever they want and you are also free to speak up. Just make sure you do so respectfully and only over the phone. No email! The offer letter is the only documentation you will need. The conversation will, very likely, go one of two ways:

1. The company either moves the salary up a little or to an amount that fully satisfies you.

Note: You can also get creative and ask if the company can include a sign-on bonus (or a relocation bonus, if applicable) of $2,500 to bring the number up to the midpoint of the original range, for example. The reason this is an option is because sign-on bonuses are not always counted toward a company's budgeted salary. Alternatively, you could ask for a guaranteed raise after six months or additional vacation days. Remember, you're just *asking*, not demanding. Every company is different but it's worth bringing these options to their attention.

Note 2: Some companies have standard vacation policies for all employees (i.e. three weeks for new hires, four weeks once you've been there for five years, etc.) while other companies don't even have set vacation times. Understand what is negotiable and what is not.

2. They keep their offer as is.

Let's say the company holds firm at $90K. This is where you now factor in everything about this new opportunity relative to your current situation. Are all of the pieces of this compensation package reasonable enough for you to sign the offer letter? Only you can answer that question.

Every single person's situation is completely different and you will need to weigh all of the factors yourself. Companies usually expect a signed letter within a few days, so you have time to carefully think everything over.

To further illustrate this point, here's a story of someone who was in this very situation and how she handled it.

Story: Debbie was at a miserable job. She was at a company for close to five years where the conditions became steadily worse, especially over the last two years. She had been recently promoted but her responsibilities did not change and she was growing more and more frustrated. She wanted to improve the quality of her work by expanding her assignments, but that was not going to happen in her current environment.

Leaving the company without another position lined up was not something she was comfortable doing. For close to a year, she sent out résumés and even had a few interviews while continuing to work at her current position.

A former co-worker of Debbie's alerted her to an opening at his company. He helped get her résumé to the Marketing Director and the interview process was conducted quickly. Debbie established what she was looking for in terms of compensation and vacation time during the initial phone interview.

After two rounds of in-person interviews, the company made her an offer which had both the salary and the vacation time *less* than what she was making in her current role.

What did she do?

First, she read over everything and talked to a couple of her trusted friends and family members. Then she decided to bring up her concerns with HR. After the conversation, she got a revised offer letter where the company moved the salary up a little but did not budge at all on the vacation time. The offer was now final and Debbie had a choice to make by weighing everything carefully.

During that time, Joyce, Debbie's future hiring manager, contacted her directly to discuss Debbie's concerns with the vacation time and confided in her that the two of them would work together on any extra days she may need or want. Joyce felt badly Debbie was essentially getting short-changed vacation days but she couldn't get the company to budge either.

After a few days of taking everything into consideration, Debbie accepted the company's offer. She gave her two-weeks' notice and resigned from her current company.

Why?

Because the slightly lower salary, fewer vacation days, less travel, and Joyce's effort offset her long commute and daily misery she was feeling at her current job. She also knew the conditions at her current job were likely to get worse and she wasn't committing herself to any amount of time at this new position, so she went for it.

This is what I mean by **intangibles** (#5 from our original list). For some, the lower salary and fewer vacation days would be a non-starter. While for others, the idea of working in a healthier environment with new challenges and a shorter commute carry a lot of weight. It was her decision to make and it was the right one for her.

Your salary is only part of the picture when it comes to being fairly compensated for a position. While you should never allow yourself to be grossly underpaid, potentially accepting a little less money than you were expecting to improve your overall situation could very well be the right move for you.

We're all individuals and we have to make the best decisions for ourselves. There is no one right way when it comes to doing what works best for you.

Ask Yourself One Question

To close, if we boil this entire chapter down to a single question that you should ask yourself when presented with an offer letter, it would be the following:

"Will everything about this new job (role, title, manager, etc.), including the full compensation package, bring *me* more **value** than my current job?"

It's a yes or no question that forces you to take everything into consideration. Looking at your new offer in this way will help you make the smart, well-informed choice that benefits both your professional needs and your personal situation.

We've covered a lot in these nine chapters and if your head is spinning a little, that's okay. There is no way to absorb everything in this book in one reading. Please revisit whatever sections you need, whenever you need to.

Before you go, I have one last chapter that's all about staying positive and focused during your job search and beyond.

Let's go.

10

Staying Positive Now and in the Future

You're not alone if you feel pressure and/or anxiety about finding your next job.

My hope for you after reading this book is that you now have a much better handle on the whole process as well as a sharper focus on what you need to spend your time on. There are so many uncertainties with job searching, however, many of them are out of your control and therefore should not be occupying your time and your thoughts.

Make the Effort

The route to landing a new job is not set up in your favor and you need to make the extra effort, sometimes daily, to stay positive and focused so you can find the next opportunity that is right for you.

The last thing you want to do is take the easy way out just so you don't have to job search anymore. If you wind up taking "anything," then there is a likelihood you will be unhappy at the new job after only a few months or less. Of course, that job could also work out, but is rolling the dice on that prospect really in your best interest?

Only <u>you</u> know what you want to do next and what's important to you. Don't let outdated advice and fearmongers shake your confidence with their views and opinions. You have complete control over who you deal with and who you ignore.

Additionally, never forget that you have an enormous amount of value to bring to a deserving organization. The key is to now proactively find the right people on the inside, give yourself a chance to meet with them, and then decide if the opportunity makes sense.

Job opportunities that excite you and jobs that pay you a fair salary and benefits are not mutually exclusive. You are allowed to have the job you want that also lets you grow professionally and provide for your family.

20 Points

To conclude this book, I want to leave you with a list to revisit whenever you need it, especially when times are tough. Some of these points were mentioned in earlier chapters and some you will see here for the first time. These have helped me in the past and I know they will help you, too.

1. Don't compare yourself to anyone else

You don't know everyone's story and situation and it doesn't matter. Your friends and colleagues are all on their own personal journeys and so are you. Wish them well and focus on *your* next steps.

2. Take care of yourself

Exercise at least several times a week. This can be as simple as a ten-minute routine you do at home. The point is to move your body and break a sweat.

- Eat well.

- Get enough sleep.

- Get outside in the fresh air.

- Laugh. Read funny books. Watch comedies or stand-up comedy.

Looking for a new job is stressful and is even more difficult if you're sick. Stay healthy.

3. Get together with people

Don't go through it alone. Reach out to friends, former co-workers, or classmates for coffee or lunch. Good friends will lend an ear and provide motivation. While they may not be able to help you directly, their support will still go a long way.

4. Attend networking events

Your school's alumni association, meetup.com, and other websites have lots of events and are a great place to make a new contact or two. You never know where one meeting could lead.

5. Add variety to your day

If you are currently out of work, do not spend eight hours a day job searching. You'll get burned out. Mix it up to stay motivated...and sane.

Take some time each day to read the newspaper, different magazines, online articles, and books on people or topics that interest you. You can get all of this information for free at your public library. It's a great resource. Take advantage of it.

6. Volunteer

Seek out opportunities where you can give back to your community. This will help you clear your head and refocus while making a positive impact.

7. Update your résumé every six months

This benefits you in three main ways:

One, updating your résumé serves as a check to ensure your current position is providing adequate growth for you. If you cannot add a meaningful bullet point to your current role, then you need to take a closer look at your current situation.

Two, if you decide to start job searching while you continue to work, then you can jump right into the process as your résumé will be updated.

Three, if you are let go suddenly or quit, then you won't be panicked, you'll be prepared. You can immediately move forward and not dwell on your old job. You'll have an updated résumé and the steps needed to find the next move in your career.

8. Do a little bit to advance your situation each day

If you are currently working and looking to get out, then you need to start incorporating small steps into your daily routine to make this happen. Start with 20 minutes a day, either before or after work (or during work if you can do so safely), and start making lists and gathering information about companies that either have jobs posted or that simply interest you.

If you make this a routine, then it will not feel as daunting and after one full week, you will have spent *over two hours* focused on your job search. You can get a lot done in that amount of time.

What's even better is you will start to generate momentum and motivation to keep going because you will notice your job search and overall situation starting to take a positive turn.

9. Fill any knowledge gaps

Regardless of where you are in your job search (even if you haven't started yet), assess your skills and any areas where you might be lacking. If you want or need to get stronger in certain subjects, seek out resources both online and at your local bookstore or library. There are so many quality online courses, several of which are either free or inexpensive, that will allow you to learn at your own pace.

10. Think of where you want to go in the longer term

There's a very good chance you have an idea of where you want your career to go over the next five years or so. Keep that perspective handy and realize your very next job may be a stepping stone to a future opportunity that will help lead you toward your larger goal.

11. Set parameters for your job search, but be open too

Focus on where you want to work. Consider the commute, the hours you're willing to work, what type of organization, what size organization, etc. If an opportunity comes up where you possibly need to make concessions, then you can make them at that time. Also, you may have an opportunity that looks interesting but isn't necessarily what you are focusing on. At a minimum, be open to it and assess whether it will help you move toward your professional goals.

12. Watch the signs

They are everywhere.

13. Do not put up with nonsense

If a company "ghosts" you or treats you unprofessionally during the process, acknowledge that it's their loss, not yours, and move on.

Remember, you're just looking for one good fit.

14. Keep practicing your interviewing skills

It's possible you'll have gaps of time in between interviews. Make the effort to consistently rehearse answers to common interview questions to stay sharp. You can practice with friends or out loud by yourself. This will help take some of the pressure off of you when the next interview comes around...which it will.

15. If you can do 50% of what is posted in a job description, then go ahead and apply

Most job descriptions are written in the hopes that the ideal candidate will apply and be able to fulfill every requirement a company has. This is almost never the case. Companies make concessions all the time, so don't let a job description dissuade you from applying. Good companies and good managers want good people. Skills and processes can all be taught. Be confident in your abilities and don't be afraid to go after a position.

16. Mail your résumé and cover letter, then apply online

Do what so many job seekers are not doing and get your résumé and cover letter right onto the hiring manager's desk. Mailing your information will also ensure all of the effort you put in to these documents does not go to waste.

17. Focus on one question when it comes to a final offer

When the final offer is in front of you, ask yourself:

"Will everything about this new job (role, title, manager, etc.), including the full compensation package, bring *me* more **value** than my current job?"

Remember, value includes the work, salary, benefits, vacation time, remote work, travel, and all of the intangibles unique to you.

18. Be selfish

Focus on *you* and realize you have a ton to offer a deserving organization. Do not let yourself get discouraged and do not let any company or individual make you doubt the reasons that got you to this point. Anyone who doesn't have your best interests at heart, doesn't get a say on your next career move.

19. Take control of your career

Do whatever you need to do to keep moving toward your personal and professional short and long-term goals.

20. Get the right job

It's out there.

I truly wish you all the best.

Appendix

Résumé Checklist

☐ Your name is the biggest font and goes in the top center of the page

☐ City/Town, State only; not your street address

☐ One phone number, email address, and your LinkedIn URL

☐ Use hyperlinks for your email and LinkedIn URL

☐ Test the hyperlinks to ensure they are working properly

☐ Summary detailing who you are, what you enjoy/are good at, possibly including a recent achievement, and what you are looking to do next (4-5 sentences only)

☐ Work history in reverse chronological order

☐ Company names in bold

☐ Job titles in bold and italics

☐ Short sentence about the company and your role in general terms

☐ Focus on achievements and accomplishments (some daily tasks are okay, but don't overdo it)

☐ Write in longer sentence fragments or full sentences

☐ Use pronouns and articles

☐ Education, Skills, and Interests at the bottom

☐ Education at the top if you are a recent graduate

☐ Evenly spaced right and left margins (about an inch on both sides)

☐ Bullet points vertically in line

☐ Consistent font type and size

☐ Check spelling

☐ Check punctuation

☐ Define all acronyms (if necessary)

☐ Overall look (is it inviting to read or does it look too crowded or weak?)

- One page max, generally, if you have been working less than 10 years, otherwise 2 pages max

Some Behavioral Questions

Tell me about a time when you ...

- disagreed with someone at work and had to work through it.
- took a current process and improved it.
- made a mistake and then went about correcting it.
- led a team or an initiative.
- handled a difficult situation.
- multi-tasked.
- worked well under pressure.
- persuaded someone to try something new/see something your way.

Some Additional Questions

- What made you apply for this job?
- What have you learned about our company?
- Why are you looking for a job now?
- What is your greatest career accomplishment so far?
- How does this job relate to other jobs you've held?
- If you are hired for this job, how will you approach assignments?

Work with Me

If you'd like to work with me, please visit my website, or my LinkedIn page, and drop me a line. I offer a free 15-minute phone consultation to all new clients.

www.jeffmagnusonconsulting.com

www.linkedin.com/in/jmagnuson

Acknowledgements

This book would not have been possible without the help and support of the following people:

- ✓ Chris Perez
- ✓ Cara Strickler
- ✓ Aaron Strickler
- ✓ Jennifer Brown
- ✓ Audrey Magnuson
- ✓ Bradley Heller
- ✓ Jordan Eagles
- ✓ Kostis Pavlou

Thank you to all of my clients for trusting me to help you.

Thank YOU for choosing this book to help you on your professional journey.

If you liked this book...

Please help other readers easily find it by leaving a review on *Amazon* or *Goodreads*. Thank you so much.

www.amazon.com/author/jeffmagnuson

————————

Jeff Magnuson is a career consultant, specializing in all areas of business, and an author. He earned his BA from Rutgers University and his MBA from the University of North Carolina at Chapel Hill. He lives in northern New Jersey. You can view his full list of consulting services at **www.jeffmagnusonconsulting.com.**

Made in the USA
Middletown, DE
22 January 2021